i

STARGROUP SPOTLIGHTS

THE DEMOCRATIC PARTY

StarGroup International, Inc.
West Palm Beach, Florida

Published 2004

FIRST EDITION

Concept & supervision by Brenda Star
Edited by Shawn McAllister
Research by Cheryl Kravetz
Book design by Mel Abfier
Cover design by Ida Perez

Designed and produced by StarGroup International, Inc.
(561) 547-0667
www.stargroupinternational.com

Printed in the United States of America

Library of Congress Cataloging-in-Publication Data pending.

Part of the StarGroup Spotlights Series
StarGroup Spotlights: The DEMOCRATIC Party
ISBN 1-884886-78-7

Book Orders

- One to fifty copies may be ordered online at:
  www.stargroupspotlights.com
- This book is also available for bulk purchases and customized printings (interior & exterior):
  www.stargroupinternational.com
- Donations for distribution of this publication can be made through the 501(C)3 Star Foundation:
  561-547-0667

STARGROUP SPOTLIGHTS

THE DEMOCRATIC PARTY

STARGROUP
INTERNATIONAL INC

Additional books by StarGroup Book Division

StarGroup Spotlights:

• Celebrating AMERICA	2004
• The REPUBLICAN PARTY	2004
• Understanding DIVERSITY	2004
• Saving The ENVIRONMENT	2004
• The Value of MENTORING	2004
• The Evolution of U.S. MONEY	2004
• Why Children Need MUSIC	2004
• READING With Your Child	2004
• Staying in SCHOOL	2004

Upcoming:

StarGroup Spotlights:

- Good HEALTH for CHILDREN
- Good HEALTH for ADULTS
- Healthy NUTRITION
- PARENTING
- WEIGHT CONTROL
- How AMERICA'S LEGAL SYSTEM Works
- CITIZENSHIP

Currently in Print by StarGroup:

- 101 Reasons To READ To Your Child (First Edition 2000
- 101 Reasons To READ With Your Child (Second Edition 2001)
- 101 Reasons To Be A PROUD AMERICAN (2001)

Table of Contents

The History of the Party

Thomas Jefferson founded the Democratic Party in 1792 as a congressional caucus to fight for the Bill of Rights and against the elitist Federalist Party. In 1798, the "party of the common man" was officially named the Democratic-Republican Party and in 1800 elected Jefferson as the first Democratic President of the United States. Jefferson served two distinguished terms and was followed by James Madison in 1808. Madison strengthened America's armed forces, helping reaffirm American independence by defeating the British in the War of 1812. James Monroe was elected president in 1816 and led the nation through a time commonly known as "The Era of Good Feeling" in which Democratic-Republicans served with little opposition.

The election of John Quincy Adams in 1824 was highly contested and led to a four-way split among Democratic-Republicans. A result of the split was the emergence of Andrew Jackson as a national leader. The war hero, generally considered, along with Jefferson, one of the founding fathers of the Democratic Party, organized his supporters to a degree unprecedented in American history. The Jacksonian Democrats created the national convention process, the party platform, and reunified the Democratic Party with Jackson's victories in 1828 and

1832. The Party held its first National Convention in 1832 and nominated President Jackson for his second term. In 1844, the National Convention simplified the Party's name to the Democratic Party.

In 1848, the National Convention established the Democratic National Committee, now the longest running political organization in the world. The Convention charged the DNC with the responsibility of promoting "the Democratic cause" between the conventions and preparing for the next convention.

As the 19th Century came to a close, the American electorate changed more and more rapidly. The Democratic Party embraced the immigrants who flooded into cities and industrial centers, built a political base by bringing them into the American mainstream, and helped create the most powerful economic engine in history. Democratic Party leader William Jennings Bryan led a movement of agrarian reformers and supported the right of women's suffrage, the progressive graduated income tax and the direct election of Senators. As America entered the 20th Century, the Democratic Party became dominant in local urban politics.

In 1912, Woodrow Wilson became the first Democratic president of the 20th Century. Wilson led the country through World War I, fought for the League of Nations, established the Federal Reserve Board, and passed the first labor and child welfare laws.

A generation later, Franklin Roosevelt was elected president running on the promise of a New Deal. Roosevelt pulled America out of the Depression by looking beyond the Democratic base and energizing citizens around the belief that their government could actively assist them in times of need. Roosevelt's New Deal brought water to

California's Central Valley, electrified Appalachia and saved farms across the Midwest. The Civilian Conservation Corps, the WPA and Social Security all brought Americans into the system, freeing us from fear, giving us a stake in the future, making the nation stronger.

With the election of Harry Truman, Democrats began the fight to bring down the final barriers of race and gender. Truman integrated the military and oversaw the reconstruction of Europe by establishing the Marshall Plan and the North Atlantic Treaty Organization. Truman's leadership paved the way for civil rights leaders who followed.

In the 1960s, President John F. Kennedy challenged an optimistic nation to build on its great history. Kennedy proclaimed a New Frontier and dared Americans to put a man on the moon, created the Peace Corps, and negotiated a treaty banning atmospheric testing of nuclear weapons. Lyndon Johnson followed Kennedy's lead and worked to pass the Civil Rights Act and Voting Rights Act. Kennedy and Johnson worked together to end the practice of segregation in many southern states. Following Kennedy's assassination, Johnson declared a War on Poverty and formed a series of Great Society programs, including the creation of Medicare, ensuring that older Americans would receive quality health care.

In 1976, Jimmy Carter was elected president, helping to restore the nation's trust in government following the Watergate scandal. Among other things, Carter negotiated the historic Camp David peace accords between Egypt and Israel.

In 1992, Arkansas Governor Bill Clinton was elected the 42nd President of the United States. President Clinton ran on the promise of a New Covenant for America's forgotten working families. After twelve years of Republican presidents, America faced record budget deficits, high unemployment, and increasing crime. President Clinton's policies put people first and resulted in the longest period of economic expansion in peacetime history. The Deficit Reduction Act of 1993, passed by both the House and Senate without a single Republican vote, put America on the road to fiscal responsibility and led to the end of perennial budget deficits. Having inherited a $290 billion deficit in 1992, President Clinton's last budget was over $200 billion in surplus. The Clinton/Gore Administration was responsible for reducing unemployment to its lowest level in decades and reducing crime to its lowest levels in a generation. In 1996, President Clinton became the first Democratic president reelected since Roosevelt. In 1998, Democrats became the first party controlling the White House to gain seats in Congress during the sixth year of a president's term since 1822.

In the 2000 elections, Vice President Al Gore won the popular vote for President by more than 500,000 votes although he lost the election due to the electorial vote count. In 2001, Democrats regained control of the Senate under Majority Leader Tom Daschle.

History of the Democratic Party Provided
by the Democratic National Committee

Fun Facts and Trivia

- The Democratic Party was founded in 1792 by Thomas Jefferson as a congressional caucus to fight for the Bill of Rights and against the elitist Federalist Party.

- In 1798, the "party of the common man" was officially named the Democratic-Republican Party and in 1800 elected Jefferson as the first Democratic President of the United States.

- There were actually seven presidents before George Washington, known historically as the "Presidents under the Articles of Confederation" with the official title of "President of the United States in Congress Assembled." The first was John Hanson (1781-82), and the next six presidents were Elias Boudinot (1783), Thomas Mifflin (1784), Richard Henry Lee (1785), Nathan Gorman (1786), Arthur St. Clair (1787), and Cyrus Griffin (1788). There were sixteen Presidents of the Continental Congress, but John Hanson, the ninth, was the first to serve as President under the Articles of Confederation and the first to hold the title "President of the United States."

- Four U.S. Presidents were members of the Democratic-Republican Party and fourteen were members of the Democratic Party.

- Thomas Jefferson (1801-1809) was the first president to be inaugurated in Washington, D.C. Bad weather delayed the arrival of a new $6,000 carriage and an expensive velvet suit, forcing him to walk to his inauguration in 1801 wearing a gray homespun suit.

- Jefferson enjoyed exploring caves and was the country's first-known speleologist.

- The dome on Thomas Jefferson's home, Monticello, conceals a billiards room. In Jefferson's day, billiards were illegal in Virginia.

- Jefferson's 6,500-volume book collection was purchased by The Library of Congress in 1815 for $23,950 to replace the collection that had been burned by the British.

- Jefferson's Vice President, Aaron Burr, the first vice president chosen by the House, was dropped from the ticket and later arrested for treason and murder.

- James Madison served as Secretary of State under Thomas Jefferson.

- Jefferson was a widower, so Madison's wife, Dolley, served as White House hostess during his administration.

- Jefferson was the third President of the United States and the man who wrote, "We hold these truths to be self-evident, that all men are created equal, that they are endowed by their Creator with certain unalienable Rights, that among these are Life, Liberty, and the pursuit of Happiness." He died almost broke on July 4, 1826.

- Clarence Darrow, lawyer and author (1857-1938), once observed, "When I was a boy I was told that anybody could become President. Now I'm beginning to believe it."

- There was one individual who served in the position of president without ever being sworn in. In 1849, March 4th, the day the new president, Zachary Taylor, would have taken office, fell on a Sunday. President James Polk left on schedule, but Taylor did not take the oath until the next day. So Missourian David Rice Atchinson, president pro tempore of the Senate, "held down the fort" until Taylor was sworn in. Atchinson neither started a war nor raised any taxes. He just left quietly after 24 hours.

- Daniel Webster, a U.S. congressman in the nineteenth century, wanted more than anything else to be President of the United States. He was offered the job of vice-president by William Henry Harrison, but turned it down. Then Harrison died in office. Again Webster was offered the vice-presidency, by Zachary Taylor, but declined. Taylor died in office. Webster never did become President.

- Originally, electors did not vote separately for President and Vice President. They were not permitted to indicate which votes were for President and which votes were for Vice President. It was presumed that the second most qualified person would become Vice President. It did not presume that party politics would exist.

- James Madison (1809-1827) was the smallest of all the presidents. He was only 5'4" tall and weighed less than 100 pounds.

- While she was First Lady in 1812, Dolley Madison rescued Gilbert's famous portrait of George Washington from the burning White House when the British torched it. That portrait is the only remaining possession from the original building.

- James Madison and Zachary Taylor were second cousins.

- Elected President in 1808, Madison was the first president to wear long trousers. Those before him wore knee breeches.

- Madison's last words were: "I always talk better lying down."

- James Monroe (1817-1825) became president after more than 40 years of public service and is best known for the Monroe Doctrine warning European countries not to interfere with the free nations of the Western Hemisphere.

- The White House was painted white the year Monroe became president.

- Monroe received every electoral vote but one in the election of 1820, because a New Hampshire delegate wanted Washington to be the only president elected unanimously.

- James Monroe died in 1831 and was the third president to die on July 4 after leaving office. The other two were John Adams and Thomas Jefferson who both died on Independence Day in 1826.

- John Quincy Adams (1825-1829) was the first president to have his photo taken (April 13, 1843).

- Andrew Jackson (1829-1837) was the first man to be nominated for president at a Democratic National Convention.

- Andrew Jackson was the only president who served in both the Revolutionary War and the War of 1812.

- Jackson was the first president to ride on a railroad train.

- Jackson was known to have a temper and was involved in many duels. He once intervened in an argument between a friend and a Mr. Charles Dickinson in 1806, after which on several occasions Mr. Dickinson made some provocative and insulting remarks about him and his wife, including a statement in the Nashville Review calling him "worthless scoundrel, ... a poltroon and a coward." Jackson challenged Dickinson, an accomplished marksman, to a duel, during which Dickinson shot him in the chest before he was able to get off a shot, the bullet lodging inches from his heart. Instead of firing his shot into the air, as was customary, Jackson then slowly raised his pistol while clutching his chest, aimed, and pulled the trigger, fatally wounding Dickinson. The bullet in Jackson's chest could not be removed and never properly healed. The abscesses around the slug caused him much discomfort and pain for the remainder of his life, which lasted another 39 years.

- Jackson's vice president, Martin Van Buren, presided over the Senate wearing a pair of pistols as a precaution against the frequent outbursts of violence.

- Jackson's wife, Rachel, smoked a pipe.

- The first national nominating convention was held in Baltimore, Maryland in 1832. Since then, 9 Democratic National Conventions and 1 Republican National Convention have been held there. The city that has hosted the most national political conventions is Chicago: 11 Democratic and 14 Republican.

- Martin Van Buren (1837-1841) was the first president who was born a U.S. citizen.

- Van Buren was one of the founders of the Democratic Party.

- The Democratic Party adopted its first platform in 1840.

- James K. Polk (1845-1849) was the only president in American history who managed to keep all of his campaign promises during his tenure. During the 1844 campaign, he made 5 promises: to acquire California from Mexico, to settle the Oregon dispute, to lower the tariff, to establish a sub-treasury, and to retire from the office after 4 years. When he left office, his campaign promises had all been fulfilled.

- Polk was the first "dark horse" presidential nominee in U.S. history.

- The first gaslight was turned on in the White House during Polk's administration on December 29, 1848.

- Polk was the first president to have an official photo taken while in office (1849). Previous office holders had portraits made.

- Franklin Pierce (1853-1857) was the youngest and is said to be the most handsome president up to that time when he took office.

- Pierce was the first president to have a Christmas tree in the White House.

- Jefferson Davis, later the President of the Confederate States of America, was a Senator from Mississippi and Secretary of War when he won a handful of votes at the Democratic conventions in 1848, 1852, and 1860.

- The 1860 Democratic convention took place during two different blocks of days in two different cities: Charleston, South Carolina and Baltimore, Maryland.

- James Buchanan (1857-1861) is the only U.S. President who never married, although he was engaged to be married when he was 28. His fiancée broke off the engagement because of untrue rumors. When she died young, a heart-broken and grief-stricken Buchanan vowed never to marry, and to this day is the only president to remain a bachelor his entire life.

- Buchanan reputedly had the neatest handwriting of all the presidents.

- Buchanan was President Polk's secretary of state. He was also appointed minister to Russia in President Jackson's first term, to which Jackson explained, "It was as far as I could send him out of my sight, and where he could do the least harm. I would have sent him to the North Pole if we had kept a minister there!"

- Queen Victoria of England sent the first Atlantic cable to President Buchanan.

- Following the walkout of nine delegations at the 1860 Democratic National Convention in Charleston, South Carolina, the convention reconvened six weeks later in Baltimore, Maryland.

- Dark Horse Abraham Lincoln was elected because the north and south split into two factions at the 1860 Democratic National Convention. Stephen Douglas represented Northern Democrats and John Breckenridge represented Southern Democrats on the ticket, allowing the new Republican Party to emerge victorious.

- President Andrew Johnson (1865-1869) stood trial for impeachment in 1868. The impeachment vote did not pass in the Senate.

- When he died, Andrew Johnson was buried wrapped in a U.S. flag with his well-worn copy of the Constitution under his head.

- The Democrats' shortest convention was held in 1872 and only lasted six hours.

- The 1876 convention in St. Louis, Missouri was the first Democratic National Convention to be held west of the Mississippi River.

- Democrat Samuel Jones Tilden of New York won the presidential election of 1876, but a 15-member panel overturned the decision in favor of Republican candidate Rutherford B. Hayes.

- In 1880, James Garfield became the first presidential candidate to spend more than one million dollars on his campaign.

- Garfield was the last person to be elected to the Presidency directly from the House of Representatives.

- Before he was able to cast a vote himself at the age of 19, Grover Cleveland worked on Democrat James Buchanan's successful bid for president in 1856 and ironically became the next Democrat to win the White House 28 years later in 1884.

- Grover Cleveland (1885-1889) was the only Democratic president to serve in the White House during the 44 years from 1869 until 1913.

- Cleveland was the only president to serve two nonconsecutive terms in office. He was elected president in 1884, voted out of office in 1888, and was voted back in 1892.

- Grover Cleveland's vice president, Adlai Stevenson (1893-1897), had a grandson of the same name who was nominated for the presidency by the Democratic Party at the 1952 and 1956 conventions.

- In 1912, Woodrow Wilson (1913-1921) defeated two presidents in one election, incumbent President William Howard Taft, and former President Theodore Roosevelt.

- Woodrow Wilson is the only U.S. president to this day to receive an earned Ph.D. His degree was in History from Johns Hopkins University.

- President Wilson completed the Panama Canal by setting off explosives through a signal by wire from New York City. The canal's excavation occurred from each coast working inland toward a connecting point with the final short segment being cleared by explosives detonated by the president.

- Woodrow Wilson's vice president Thomas Marshall once remarked, "What this country needs is a good five-cent cigar," to which American Humorist Will Rogers replied, "Our country has plenty of good five-cent cigars, but the trouble is they charge fifteen cents for them."

- Woodrow Wilson is the only president buried in Washington, D.C. He is buried at the Washington Cathedral.

- Ohio Governor James Cox received the presidential nomination of his party at the 1920 Democratic National Convention in San Francisco, CA. His running mate was the Secretary of the Navy at the time, Franklin D. Roosevelt.

- Laura Clay was the first woman to receive a vote for either president or vice president at the 1920 Democratic National Convention in San Francisco.

- Democrats held the longest convention in American history in 1924, which took 103 ballots in nine days spread out over a 16-day period, to nominate John W. Davis.

- As a direct result of the two-thirds rule, Democratic Conventions went 46 ballots over eight days in 1912 and 44 ballots in nine days in 1924.

- The first journalist to receive a convention vote was Will Rogers in 1924. Although usually thought of as a humorist and performer, Rogers wrote a regular syndicated column and covered a number of conventions with ordinary press credentials from the press gallery.

- Franklin D. Roosevelt (1933-1945) was elected to four terms as President from 1933 to 1945 and had three Vice Presidents serve during his tenure: John Nance Garner (1933-1941), Henry Wallace (1941-1945), Harry Truman (1945).

- In 1933, for the first time in history, all the members of the Electoral College were invited to a presidential inauguration to witness Franklin Roosevelt take the oath of office.

- President Roosevelt threatened to resign the nomination for President of the United States in 1940 if the democratic national convention did not choose Henry Wallace to be his running mate.

- The presidential inauguration date was moved to January 20 during the Franklin Roosevelt presidency in 1937.

- The first president to appear on black & white television was Franklin Delano Roosevelt on April 30, 1939 at the opening ceremonies for the World's Fair.

- The first president to fly in an airplane while in office was Franklin Delano Roosevelt in 1943.

- FDR was the first U.S. President to have a presidential aircraft. He only flew on the specially equipped Douglas DC-4, nicknamed "The Sacred Cow," once; to travel to the Yalta Conference during World War II. It was equipped with an elevator so that the president could board the plane while remaining in his wheelchair. The aircraft currently is on display at the USAF museum in Dayton, Ohio.

- FDR was the most superstitious president. He traveled continually but never left on a Friday. He also wouldn't sit at the same table that held thirteen other people.

- By the time FDR's mother died, in 1941, FDR had presided over at least eight annual budgets of the largest fiscal entity on earth. Yet during her lifetime, Sara Delano Roosevelt would not entrust her son to manage the family's money because she did not think her son up to the task.

- The first television coverage of political conventions was in 1940.

- Socialist Norman Thomas, one of the founders of the American Civil Liberties Union, ran for President as the Socialist Party candidate six times in every election from 1928 to 1948. Although he never polled more than 884,000 popular votes in any one election, his influence was strong enough to cause elected Presidents like FDR to implement some of his programs, such as unemployment compensation and Social Security.

- Democratic candidates Grover Cleveland, William Jennings Bryan and Franklin D. Roosevelt received the presidential nomination three times each.

- At 71 years of age, Alben Barkley was the oldest Vice President to assume office when he was sworn in with Harry Truman (1945-1953) in 1949.

- Harry Truman's middle name was just 'S.' It is not an

abbreviation, just an initial. His parents could not decide between two different names beginning with S.

- Harry S. Truman was the first president to give a televised address from the White House on October 5, 1947.

- When Harry Truman left office in 1952 he drove himself back to Missouri in his own car.

- There was a 12-year stretch where both political parties consecutively held their conventions in the same cities. The 1944, 1948 and 1952 political conventions were held in the same cities. In 1944, Chicago hosted both parties; in 1948, Philadelphia hosted the conventions, and in 1952, Chicago held both conventions.

- Alben Barkley, vice president under Harry S. Truman (1949-1953), delivered the keynote address to two Democratic Conventions twelve years apart, the first in 1936 and second in 1948.

- Three states — Louisiana, South Carolina and Virginia — refused to agree to a party loyalty pledge at the 1952 Democratic National Convention, resulting in their credentials being brought into question.

- In 1956, Senator John F. Kennedy narrowly lost a bid to Estes Kefauver, to become Adlai Stevenson's vice-presidential running mate on the Democratic ticket.

- The youngest elected president was John F. Kennedy (1961-1963) at 43. The youngest president to be inaugurated was Theodore Roosevelt at 42, following the assassination of William McKinley.

- The controversial "unit rule," allowing a state delegation's majority to cast all of that delegation's votes, was abolished at the 1968 Democratic National

Convention in Chicago. The controversial unit rule and the two-thirds rule (abolished in 1968), were used by the Democratic Party but were never used by the Republicans.

- Lyndon Johnson resigned his Texas Senate seat and the position of Senate Majority Leader after winning election as Vice President along with John Kennedy on the 1960 Presidential ticket.

- John F. Kennedy (1961-1963) was the first, and to date the only, Catholic elected to the U.S. presidency.

- Kennedy was the last person to date to be elected directly from the Senate to the Presidency.

- JFK was the first Navy veteran to become President. Since Kennedy, every President has been a Navy veteran, except Reagan, who was an Army veteran, and Clinton who didn't serve at all.

- Lyndon Johnson (1963-1969) received his party's nomination on his 56th birthday at the 1964 Democratic National Convention.

- Lyndon Johnson had no Vice President from November 1963 through January 1965.

- Daniel K. Inouye is the only representative from Hawaii to have ever delivered the keynote address to a Democratic National Convention. It occurred at the 1968 Democratic National Convention in Chicago.

- In 1972 both the Democratic and Republican National Conventions were held in Miami Beach, Florida.

- Archie Bunker, the lovable bigot of the 1970s sitcom "All in the Family" received a vote for vice president at the 1972 Democratic Convention apparently as a protest against the liberal proceedings.

- The 1972 Democratic convention was the first convention in history with more than 3,000 delegates. The eight largest conventions in history are all Democratic affairs.

- Shirley Chisholm was the first African-American woman to seek the presidential nomination from a national political party at the 1972 Democratic National Convention in Miami Beach.

- Thomas Eagleton resigned the Democratic Vice Presidential nomination in 1972. Presidential nominee George McGovern replaced him with Sargent Shriver. Since 1944, (56 years and 14 elections) Sargent Shriver is the only Democratic Vice Presidential nominee who did not serve in Congress at any point in his career. All other nominees served in either the U.S. Senate or House.

- Jimmy Carter (1977-1981) was the only Democratic President who attended a U.S. military academy, Annapolis.

- Carter was the first president born in a hospital.

- The Vice President did not live in his official home, the Naval Observatory, until Walter Mondale moved into the old Naval Observatory in 1977.

- Geraldine Ferraro became the first woman to appear on a major ticket when Walter Mondale selected her to join his campaign in 1984 as the Vice Presidential nominee.

- Chicago, Illinois hosted the most political conventions, both Democratic and Republican, with 25, followed by Baltimore, Maryland with 10, and Philadelphia, Pennsylvania with 8.

- Arizona Congressman and member of the Basketball Hall of Fame Morris King Udall gave the keynote address to the 1980 Democratic National Convention in New York City.

- Civil rights activist, reverend and former presidential candidate Jesse Jackson has addressed every Democratic Convention since 1984.

- Carol Moseley-Braun was the first and only African-American female to ever serve in the U.S. Senate (1993-1999). She ran unsuccessfully for the Democratic presidential nomination in 2004.

- Former New York Governor Mario Cuomo gave then Governor Bill Clinton the nickname "The Comeback Kid" when he formally nominated the future president at the 1992 Democratic National Convention.

- Bill Clinton (1993-2001) was the first left-handed American president to serve two terms.

- 22.2 million new jobs were created during the Clinton Administration, the most jobs ever created under a single Administration.

- President Clinton stood trial for impeachment. The Senate acquitted him on Feb 12, 1999.

- Joe Lieberman of Connecticut was the first Jewish American to be nominated for Vice President of the United States.

- All Vice Presidents of the 20th Century who succeeded to the Presidency won their party nominations for President and all Vice Presidents of the 20th Century who succeeded to the Presidency won the Presidency, with the exception of Republican Gerald Ford.

- From 1928 to 2004, (73 years and 18 elections), only two Democratic Vice Presidential nominees did not serve in Congress at any point in his or her career.

(Henry Wallace, 1940, and Sargent Shriver, 1972.) All other nominees once served in either the U.S. Senate or House.

- Out of the 791 people who have received votes at conventions, 29 have been women, 27 of which were Democrats. Geraldine Ferraro got more votes than any other woman. Next in line is activist Sissy Farenthold, with over 400 votes. Farenthold made a serious bid for delegates during the chaotic 1972 Democratic vice-presidential balloting. Third is former congresswoman Shirley Chisholm, the first African-American woman to run for President.

- 791 people have received votes at major party conventions since the 1830s, 503 of which were Democrats.

- Two Democratic Presidents won the Nobel Peace Prize: Woodrow Wilson in 1919 and Jimmy Carter in 2002.

- There have been two sets of presidents who were father and son: John Adams and John Quincy Adams, and George Bush and George W. Bush. Other presidents who were related: William H. Harrison and Benjamin Harrison (grandfather and grandson); James Madison and Zachary Taylor (second cousins); and Theodore Roosevelt and Franklin D. Roosevelt (fifth cousins).

- Beginning in 1840, and in each consecutive 20-year presidential administration through 1960, the incumbent President has died in office. The "Twenty Year Curse" was supposedly cast upon the presidency at the hands of an unknown Indian Chief.

1840 - William Henry Harrison...pneumonia

1860 - Abraham Lincoln...assassination

1880 - James Garfield...assassination

1900 - William McKinley...assassination

1920 - Warren Harding...heart failure

1940 - Franklin Roosevelt...cerebral hemorrhage

1960 - John Kennedy...assassinated

1980 - Ronald Reagan...Although he did not die in office, he was shot and nearly killed by an assassin.

- Eight presidents have died in office (four by assassination):

  - William Henry Harrison, 9th president (1841), died April 4, 1841 from pneumonia.

  - Zachary Taylor, 12th president (1849-50), died July 9, 1850 from food poisoning or cholera.

  - Abraham Lincoln, 16th president (1861-65), died April 15, 1865 by assassination.

  - James Abram Garfield, 20th president (1881), died September 19, 1881 from blood poisoning resulting from doctors probing for an assassin's bullet with non-sterile instruments.

  - William McKinley, 25th president (1897-1901), died September 14, 1901 by assassination.

  - Warren G. Harding, 29th president (1921-23), died August 2, 1923 from either a heart attack or a stroke depending on the source. Harding's wife refused to allow an autopsy to be performed.

  - Franklin D. Roosevelt, 32nd president (1933-45), died April 12, 1945 from a cerebral hemorrhage.

  - John F. Kennedy, 35th president (1961-63), died November 22, 1963 by assassination.

- There have been four cases thus far of Presidents who lost the popular vote but still became President. The House of Representatives awarded John Quincy Adams the presidency in 1824 even though he had not won the popular vote or the Electoral College vote (neither he nor opponent Andrew Jackson had an Electoral College majority). In 1876, Rutherford B. Hayes became President despite losing the popular vote to Samuel J. Tilden, because Hayes had a one-vote advantage in the Electoral College. In 1888, in a much more clear-cut example of a candidate losing the popular vote but winning the Electoral College vote, Benjamin Harrison was elected President over Grover Cleveland. Finally, in 2000, George W. Bush became president after losing the popular vote to Al Gore, but winning the electoral vote.

- Seven presidents have changed their names legally:

  Ulysses Simpson Grant — changed from Hiram Ulysses Grant

  Grover Cleveland — changed from Stephen Grover Cleveland

  Woodrow Wilson — changed from Thomas Woodrow Wilson

  Calvin Coolidge — changed from John Calvin Coolidge

  Dwight David Eisenhower — changed from David Dwight Eisenhower

  Gerald Rudolph Ford — changed from Leslie King, Jr. (changed when his mother remarried and his stepfather legally adopted him)

  William Jefferson Clinton — changed from William Jefferson Blythe (changed when his mother remarried and his stepfather legally adopted him).

Landmark Dates in Democratic History

1792

Organized by Thomas Jefferson as a Congressional Caucus to fight for the Bill of Rights and against the elite Federalist Party.

1798

Became the "party of the common man" and was officially called the Democratic-Republicans.

1800

Jefferson elected as the first Democratic President. Negotiated the Louisiana Purchase, which included all or parts of what would become Louisiana, Arkansas, Missouri, Iowa, North Dakota, South Dakota, Nebraska, Kansas, Wyoming, Minnesota, Oklahoma, Colorado and Montana.

1808

James Madison was elected President.

1814

Won the War of 1812. Strengthened the armed forces.

1816

James Monroe was elected President. Established the Monroe Doctrine, which sought to limit the European influence in Western Hemisphere affairs.

1824

John Quincy Adams was elected President. The Party split as four Democratic candidates ran.

1828

Andrew Jackson was elected President. Created the national convention process, the party platform, and reunified the Party on the issue of states' rights.

1937

Martin Van Buren was elected President.

1840

Officially named the Democratic Party.

1844

James Polk was elected President. Annexed the Oregon Territory. Defeated Mexico and gained the Republic of Texas and the southwestern territories.

1852

Franklin Pierce was elected President.

1856

James Buchanan was elected President.

1860

The Democratic Party formally split over slavery: Northern wing supported Stephen A. Douglas, Southern wing supported John F. Breckenridge.

1876

Samuel Tilden ran unsuccessfully for President, a predecessor of the Progressive Reformers of the 1900s.

1884

Grover Cleveland was elected President; he was also elected in 1892. Reformed the Civil Service system for government employees, reducing the number of jobs awarded on the basis of patronage.

1896

William Jennings Bryan ran unsuccessfully for President; he also ran in 1900 and 1908. Led a movement of agrarian reformers. Supported the right of women's suffrage.

Supported the progressive graduated income tax.

Supported the direct election of Senators.

1900s

Party became predominant in local urban politics.

1912

Woodrow Wilson was elected President. Led the country through World War I. Fought for the League of Nations. Established the Federal Reserve Board. Passed the first labor and child welfare laws.

1920s

Democrats were divided over the issue of Prohibition.

Alfred Smith ran for the Presidency, becoming the first Catholic candidate.

Democrats helped to establish the first primary system.

1932

Franklin Delano Roosevelt was elected President and brought the nation out of the Great Depression.

Guided us through most of World War II.

Established the Social Security System.

Established the Civilian Conservation Corps.

Reformed the national banking system.

Established the Tennessee Valley Authority.

Established the Works Progress Administration.

Formed the National Industrial Recovery Act.

1945

Harry S. Truman became President.

Established the Marshall Plan, which rebuilt Europe after World War II.

Established the Truman Doctrine, calling for U.S intervention where necessary to protect nations from communism.

Established NATO, the North Atlantic Treaty Organization.

1952

Adlai Stevenson ran unsuccessfully for President; he also ran in 1956.

1953-60

Democratic-controlled Congress passed the first civil rights legislation in 85 years.

1960

John F. Kennedy was elected President.

1961

The Peace Corps was created.

1963

Negotiated a treaty banning atmospheric testing of nuclear weapons.

John F. Kennedy was assassinated; Lyndon B. Johnson became president.

Formation of the Great Society programs and the War on Poverty.

1964

Passage of the Civil Rights Act.

1965

Creation of Medicare.

1968

Robert Kennedy was assassinated.

1976

Jimmy Carter was elected President. The Panama Canal treaties were nogotiated. The Camp David peace treaties between Egypt and Israel were negotiated.

1982

Congressional Democrats helped establish a national plan for disposal of nuclear waste.

1983

Congress, after Reagan's opposition, approved a bill establishing a national holiday honoring Dr. Martin Luther King, Jr.

1984

Democratic Presidential candidate Walter Mondale nominated Geraldine Ferraro as his running mate, the first woman vice–presidential candidate.

1985

Democratic pressure in the House led to sanctions against South Africa.

1986

November elections converted a 53-47 Republican majority in the Senate into a 55-45 Democratic advantage.

1987

The 100th Congress, led by Democrats, overrode Reagan's 1986 veto of the Clean Water bill.

1990

The Americans Disabilities Act was passed.
Head Start was expanded.
The Clean Air bill was rewritten.

1992

Bill Clinton was elected President.

1993

Passage of major legislative initiatives began, led by President Clinton and the Democratic Congress:

Economic Package: contained the largest deficit-cutting plan in history.

Student Loan Reform Act: increased access to higher education for millions.

National Service Act: helps students get tuition assistance through serving communities.

The Brady Bill: the five-day waiting period keeps convicted felons from buying guns.

National Voter Registration Act (Motor Voter): opens up access to voter registration.

Family & Medical Leave Act: offers job protection & unpaid leave during a family need.

1994

Passage of major legislative initiatives continued: The Crime Bill: the toughest and most comprehensive crime bill ever; put 100,000 more cops on our streets and combats domestic violence through the Violence Against Women Act.

School-to-Work Opportunities Act: Prepares young people for their first jobs and continuing education.

1995

President Clinton signed the Unfunded Mandates Reform Act and the Lobbying Disclosure Act of 1995.

1996

Clinton won re-election. He was the first Democrat to do so since Roosevelt.

President Clinton signed into law the Telecommunications Bill, the first reform of the communications industry since 1934.

1998

The Clinton Administration recorded the first budget surplus in decades.

1999

The Clinton Administration recorded the second budget surplus in a row.

2000

The Clinton Administration recorded the third consecutive budget surplus.

In the 2000 elections, Democrats netted four additional Senate seats, one additional House seat, and one additional gubernatorial seat. Vice President Al Gore won the popular vote for President by over 500,000 votes.

2001

Democrats regained control of the Senate under Majority Leader Tom Daschle.

Democrats swept to victory in races all across the nation, including races for Virginia Governor and Lt. Governor, New Jersey Governor, and 39 out of 42 major mayoral races including Los Angeles and Houston.

The Origin of the Donkey

When Andrew Jackson ran for president in 1828, his opponents tried to label him a "jackass" for his populist views and his slogan, "Let the people rule." Jackson, however, picked up on their name calling and turned it to his own advantage by using the donkey on his campaign posters. During his presidency, the donkey was used to represent Jackson's stubbornness when he vetoed re-chartering the National Bank.

The first time the donkey was used in a political cartoon to represent the Democratic party, it was again in conjunction with Jackson. Although in 1837 Jackson was retired, he still thought of himself as the Party's leader and was shown in the cartoon trying to get the donkey to go where he wanted it to go. The cartoon was titled "A Modern Baalim and his Ass."

Interestingly enough, the person credited with getting the donkey widely accepted as the Democratic Party's symbol probably had no knowledge of the prior associations. Thomas Nast, a famous political cartoonist, came to the United States with his parents in 1840 when he was six. He first used the donkey in an 1870 *Harper's Weekly* cartoon to represent the "Copperhead Press" kicking a dead lion, symbolizing Lincoln's Secretary of War

Edwin M. Stanton, who had recently died. Nast intended the donkey to represent an anti-war faction with whom he disagreed, but the symbol caught the public's fancy and the cartoonist continued using it to indicate some Democratic editors and newspapers.

Later, Nast used the donkey to portray what he called "Caesarism" showing the alleged Democratic uneasiness over a possible third term for Ulysses S. Grant. In conjunction with this issue, Nast helped associate the elephant with the Republican Party. Although the elephant had been connected with the Republican Party in cartoons that appeared in 1860 and 1872, it was Nast's cartoon in 1874 published by Harper's Weekly that made the pachyderm stick as the Republican's symbol. A cartoon titled "The Third Term Panic," showed animals representing various issues running away from a donkey wearing a lion's skin tagged "Caesarism." The elephant labeled "The Republican Vote," was about to run into a pit containing inflation, chaos, repudiation, etc.

By 1880 the donkey was well established as a mascot for the Democratic Party. A cartoon about the Garfield-Hancock campaign in the *New York Daily Graphic* showed the Democratic candidate mounted on a donkey, leading a procession of crusaders.

Over the years, the donkey and the elephant have become the accepted symbols of the Democratic and Republican parties. Although the Democrats have never officially adopted the donkey as a party symbol, they have used various donkey designs on publications over the years. The Republicans have actually adopted the elephant as their official symbol and use their design widely.

The Democrats think of the elephant as bungling, stupid, pompous and conservative, but the Republicans think it is dignified, strong and intelligent. On the other hand, the Republicans regard the donkey as stubborn, silly and ridiculous, but the Democrats claim it is humble, homely, smart, courageous and loveable.

Adlai Stevenson provided one of the most clever descriptions of the Republican's symbol when he said, "The elephant has a thick skin, a head full of ivory, and as everyone who has seen a circus parade knows, proceeds best by grasping the tail of its predecessor."

The Democratic Presidents

These presidents were members of the Democratic-Republican Party

Thomas Jefferson	James Madison	James Monroe	John Quincy Adams
1801-1809	1809-1817	1817-1825	1825-1829

A split in the party in 1824 caused the emergence of a new Democratic movement under the leadership of Andrew Jackson that created the national convention process, the party platform, and reunified the Democratic Party:

Andrew Jackson	Martin Van Buren	James Polk	Franklin Pierce	James Buchanan
(1829-1837)	(1837-1841)	(1845-1849)	(1853-1857)	(1857-1861)

Andrew Johnson	Grover Cleveland	Woodrow Wilson	Franklin Roosevelt	Harry S. Truman
(1865-1869)	(1885-1889 1893-1897)	(1913-1921)	(1933-1945)	(1945-1953)

John F. Kennedy	Lyndon Johnson	Jimmy Carter	Bill Clinton
(1961-1963)	(1963-1969	(1977-1981)	(1993-2001)

Thomas Jefferson

Third President
1801-1809

Born: April 13, 1743 in
Albermarle County, Virginia

Died: July 4, 1826 in Monticello,
Virginia

Married to
Martha Wayles Skelton Jefferson

Thomas Jefferson was born April 13, 1743 in Albermarle County, Virginia, the son of a planter and surveyor, from whom he inherited some 5,000 acres of land at age 14 when his father died. The land included the property where he eventually built Monticello in which he would live his entire life. His mother was a member of the Randolph family, regarded as respected members of Virginia's high society.

Following his studies at the College of William and Mary, young Jefferson studied civil and common law under the tutelage of George Wythe, who was like a surrogate father to him and a man who had one of the highest legal, legislative, and judicial minds in Virginia. Mr. Wythe was one of the leading Virginia patriots during the revolution, was a member of the House of Burgess, a signer of the Declaration of Independence, and no doubt a tremendous influence on Jefferson's views as a supporter of the new republic.

Freckled and sandy-haired, rather tall and awkward, Jefferson married the widow Martha Wayles Skelton in

1772 and took her to live in his mountaintop home, Monticello, then under construction.

Jefferson was present to hear Patrick Henry's famed speech against the Stamp Act of 1765. It was that eloquent speech that lit the flame of patriotic passion in him and drove him on his journey to serve the republic, draft the Declaration of Independence, and become the third President of the United States. He later wrote in his autobiography of the experience, "He appeared to me to speak as Homer wrote."

However, Jefferson was not a public speaker and was often referred to as the "silent member" of the Continental Congress. His strength was in his pen and the contribution of his written words clearly delineate the cause and purpose of what he believed to be the destiny of this new land.

At the age of 33, he drafted the Declaration of Independence. He continued to write many bills and historical documents, including a Virginia bill in 1786 establishing religious freedom.

He succeeded Benjamin Franklin as minister to France in 1785 and became sympathetic of the French Revolution. A short time later, while he was Secretary of State in President Washington's Cabinet, Jefferson's views of the situation in France propelled him into a heated conflict with Alexander Hamilton. This political disagreement led him to resign his State Department post in 1793 and seek to retire from politics.

However, sharp political differences erupted, from which emerged two separate parties, the Federalists and the Democratic-Republicans. Jefferson gradually assumed leadership of the Democratic-Republicans, who sympathized with the revolutionary cause in France. Attacking Federalist policies, he opposed a strong centralized Government and championed the rights of states. He wrote to a colleague during the midst of the enormous party conflict, "I have sworn upon the altar of God eternal hostility against every form of tyranny over the mind of man."

Jefferson was a reluctant candidate for President in 1796. He came within three votes of being elected. Although an opponent of President Adams, he became Vice President through a flaw in the Constitution. In 1800 the defect caused a more serious problem. The Democratic-Republicans, in attempting to name both a President and a Vice President from their own party, cast a tie vote between Jefferson and Aaron Burr. The House of Representatives had to settle the tie. Hamilton disliked both Jefferson and Burr, but nevertheless urged Jefferson's election.

The crisis in France was over when Jefferson assumed the Presidency. Even though he was growing weary of public life, he never relinquished serving the nation he loved and helped to build. He sent a naval squadron to fight Barbary pirates who were harassing American commerce in the Mediterranean. He slashed Army and Navy expenditures, cut the budget, eliminated the unpopular (in the West) tax on whiskey, and reduced the national debt by a third. Although the Constitution made no provision for the acquisition of new land, Jefferson laid aside his uncertainties over constitutionality when he had the opportunity to acquire the Louisiana Territory from Napoleon in 1803.

He became progressively preoccupied with keeping the Nation from involvement in the Napoleonic Wars during his second term, even though both England and France interfered with the neutral rights of American merchantmen. He attempted to find a solution by establishing an embargo upon American shipping, which was highly unpopular and failed miserably.

In the spring of 1809 Jefferson returned to Monticello, where he sought to "retire to my family, my books, and farms" and to contemplate such projects as his grand designs for the University of Virginia. He was said by a French nobleman to have placed his house and his mind "on an elevated situation, from which he might contemplate the universe."

He died on July 4, 1826. A short memorandum found among his possessions contained a request that his headstone bear the inscription:

HERE WAS BURIED
THOMAS JEFFERSON
AUTHOR OF THE DECLARATION
OF AMERICAN INDEPENDENCE
OF THE STATUTE OF VIRGINIA FOR RELIGIOUS
FREEDOM AND FATHER OF
THE UNIVERSITY OF VIRGINIA.

James Madison

Fourth President
1809-1817

Born: March 16, 1751 in Port Conway, King George, Virginia

Died: June 28, 1836 in Montpelier, Virginia

Married to
Dolly Payne Todd Madison

James Madison was born in 1751, the eldest of 12 children from an aristocratic family in Port Conway, Virginia. He attended the College of New Jersey (now Princeton) in 1769 and graduated in 1771, completing a four-year degree in two years. He then studied theology, history, and law, at the college as well as on his own. Appointed a member of the King George County Committee for Public Safety in Virginia at the age of 23 in 1774, he began a public career in service to his nation that would last the rest of his life. Perhaps the hardest working and most widely respected man of his day, James Madison is considered to be the Father of the U.S. Constitution. He, along with Alexander Hamilton and John Jay, wrote the Federalist essays, which contributed to the ratification of the Constitution. He objected to being singled out for his contribution, insisting that the document was not "the off-spring of a single brain ... it was the work of many heads and many hands."

In addition to participating in the framing of the Virginia Constitution in 1776, Madison served in the

Continental Congress and was a leader in the Virginia Assembly. Madison was a frequent and emphatic participant in the debates that emerged when delegates to the Constitutional Convention assembled at Philadelphia.

Madison was elected to the first House of Representatives as a Federalist & served throughout Washington's administration (1789-1797). As a trusted consultant to George Washington, Madison played a large part in forming the Departments of State, Treasury, and War. In Congress, he helped frame the Bill of Rights and enact the first revenue legislation. He stood fervently opposed to Hamilton's financial proposals, which he felt would unduly bestow wealth and power upon northern financiers. This conflict helped establish the formation of the Jeffersonian Party, which was eventually called the Democratic-Republican Party.

When Jefferson was elected President in 1801, Madison entered his Cabinet as Secretary of State. He was deeply involved in many of the federal reforms executed by Jefferson, many of which were intended to reverse the effects of federalist rule. The Napoleonic Wars erupted in Europe. As France and Britain fought with each other they often seized American merchant ships in the area. Madison highly protested to the two nations that their actions were in violation of international law. Virginia statesman John Randolph bitterly commented that the protests had the effect of "a shilling pamphlet hurled against eight hundred ships of war." Jefferson attempted to solve the situation by imposing the Embargo Act of 1807. The unpopular act did not make the belligerent nations change their ways but it did cause a depression in the United States.

Despite his involvement with the highly criticized action, Madison was elected President in 1808. Before he took office the Embargo Act was repealed.

At his inauguration, Madison appeared old and worn, prompting Washington Irving to describe him as "but a withered little apple-John." Whatever deficiencies he may have had in appearance and charm, Madison's wife Dolley compensated for them with her warmth and gaiety.

The situation in Europe grew worse. During the first year of Madison's Administration, the United States prohibited trade with both Britain and France. Congress authorized trade with both in May 1810, but directed the President to assure whichever nation agreed to accept America's view of neutral rights that trade would be forbidden to the other nation. Napoleon pretended to comply. Late in 1810, Madison discontinued communication with Great Britain. A certain faction in Congress known as the "War Hawks" pressed the President for a more militant policy. The British intervention of American seamen and the seizure of cargoes drove Madison to give in to the pressure. On June 1, 1812, he asked Congress to declare war.

The United States was a young nation and not prepared to fight. American forces were badly beaten. The British entered Washington and set fire to the White House and the Capitol. Madison was not very successful as a war president. He lost many of his followers in the War of 1812, for he was essentially a man of peace. However, he was re-elected for a second term a few months after war was declared.

Despite the overwhelming odds and substantial defeats, a few notable naval and military victories, climaxed by Gen. Andrew Jackson's triumph at New Orleans, convinced Americans that the War of 1812 had been gloriously successful. An upsurge of nationalism resulted. The New England Federalists who had opposed the war, and who had even talked secession, were so thoroughly repudiated that Federalism disappeared as a national party.

At the close of his second term Madison retired to Montpelier, his estate in Virginia. He spent the next twenty years in retirement, during which he undertook a number of projects, most notably in partnership with his friend and ally, Thomas Jefferson. He worked closely with Jefferson in establishing the University of Virginia. He also spoke out against the disruptive states' rights influences that threatened to shatter the Federal Union in the 1830s. In a note opened after his death on the morning of June 28, 1836, he stated, "The advice nearest to my heart and deepest in my convictions is that the Union of the States be cherished and perpetuated."

James Monroe

Fifth President
1817-1825

Born: April 28, 1758 in
Westmoreland County, Virginia

Died: July 4, 1831 in
New York, New York

Married to
Elizabeth Kortright Monroe

James Monroe was born on April 28, 1758 in Westmoreland County, Virginia. One of five children of Spence Monroe and Elizabeth Jones, he was raised on a small farm and walked several miles each day to attend the school of Parson Campbell, who taught him the stern moral code that he followed throughout his life.

He entered the College of William and Mary when he was 16. His father died during his first year and his uncle, Judge Joseph Jones, took over his guardianship and assumed the cost of his education. As the colonies moved closer to war with Great Britain in 1775, young Monroe found it difficult to concentrate on his studies and he left college to go to war. He became a lieutenant and took command of his unit when his captain was wounded during the Battle of Trenton before becoming wounded himself. He was named aide-de-camp to Major General Lord Stirling while recovering. Later, he fought with George Washington at Valley Forge and in 1779, as a major, was commissioned to lead a militia of Virginia regiment as a lieutenant colonel, but the unit never formed and his military career came to an end. He became an aide to the Governor of Virginia, Thomas Jefferson, where he became Jefferson's student in the study of law. Jefferson's guidance allowed him to realize what course his life would take.

In 1782, at the age of 24, Monroe was elected to the Virginia State Legislature and was the youngest member of the Executive Council. He was elected to the United States Congress that was meeting in New York City in 1783. While in New York, he met Elizabeth Kortright, whom he married on February 16, 1786, after which he resigned from Congress to settle in Fredericksburg, Virginia with his new bride. He was elected to the town council and once again to the Virginia Legislature as a member of the anti-Federalists in the Virginia Convention that ratified the Constitution before being elected United States Senator in 1790 as an advocate of Jeffersonian policies. As Minister to France in 1794-1796, he displayed strong sympathies for the French cause.

Monroe returned home in June 1797 and after two years of retirement from public office, he was elected governor of Virginia, a position that he served from 1799 until 1803. When his friend and mentor, Thomas Jefferson, became President, Monroe was sent back to France in 1803 to help Robert R. Livingston complete the negotiations for the acquisition of New Orleans and West Florida. The French Emperor, Napoleon I, offered to sell instead the entire Louisiana colony and although the Americans were not authorized to make such a large purchase, they began negotiations. In April 1803, the Louisiana Purchase was concluded, more than doubling the size of the nation. Monroe spent the next two years in useless negotiations with Britain and Spain and returned to the United States in late 1807.

Monroe returned to Virginia politics and once more served in the legislature and was elected Governor for a second time. In 1811, he became President Madison's Secretary of State and when the War of 1812 was declared, he loyally supported Madison. He served as Secretary of State throughout the war and simultaneously served as Secretary of War for the latter part. He was back in uniform at the time of the British attack on Washington and led the Maryland militia in an unsuccessful attempt to hold off the British at Bladensburg. On December 24, 1814, the Treaty of Ghent was signed ending the war. In 1815, Monroe returned to the normal peacetime duties of Secretary of State.

With the backing of President Madison, he became the Democratic-Republican choice for the Presidency in 1816 and, with little Federalist opposition, he easily won re-election in 1820.

Jefferson once said, "Monroe was so honest that if you turned his soul inside out there would not be a spot on it." A Missouri Territory application in 1819 for admission to the Union as a slave state failed. An amended bill for gradually eliminating slavery in Missouri precipitated two years of bitter debate in Congress. The Missouri Compromise bill resolved the struggle, pairing Missouri as a slave state with Maine, a free state, and barring slavery north and west of Missouri forever.

Showing an astute sense of foreign policy, Monroe proclaimed the fundamental strategy of what would become known as the Monroe Doctrine some 20 years after his death. There existed a real threat that the more conservative governments in Europe might try to aid Spain in winning back her former Latin American colonies. Monroe did not begin to formally recognize the young sister republics until 1822, after ascertaining that Congress would vote appropriations for diplomatic missions. He and Secretary of State John Quincy Adams avoided trouble with Spain until it ceded the Floridas in 1821.

Great Britain, with its powerful navy, also opposed Spain's reacquisition of Latin America and suggested that the United States join in proclaiming "hands off." Ex-Presidents Jefferson and Madison counseled Monroe to accept the offer, but Secretary Adams advised, "It would be more candid ... to avow our principles explicitly to Russia and France, than to come in as a cock-boat in the wake of the British man-of-war."

Monroe accepted Adams's advice. Not only must Latin America be left alone, he warned, but also Russia must not encroach southward on the Pacific coast. He said that "the American continents, by the free and independent condition which they have assumed and maintain, are henceforth not to be considered as subjects for future colonization by any European Power."

He was 67 years old when he turned over the presidency to John Quincy Adams. He retired to Oak Hill, Virginia, but plagued by financial worries was forced to sell his estate, Ash Lawn, to meet his debts. After his wife died, he sold Oak Hill and moved to New York City to live with his youngest daughter, Maria Hester Gouverneur and her husband. Monroe died there on July 4, 1831, the fifty-fifth anniversary of the signing of the Declaration of Independence.

John Quincy Adams

Sixth President
1825-1829

Born: July 11, 1767 in
Braintree, Massachusetts

Died: February 23, 1848, after
collapsing on the floor of the House
two days earlier

Married to
Louisa Catherine Johnson Adams

John Quincy Adams was the son of the second president of the United States, John Adams. He was born on July 11, 1767, at Braintree (now Quincy), Massachusetts. The month before his eighth birthday in 1775, he watched the Battle of Bunker Hill from the top of Penn's Hill above the family farm. He spent his early years in Europe with his father, graduated from Harvard, and entered law practice. His anti-Paine newspaper articles won him political attention. In 1794, he became minister to the Netherlands and married Louisa Catherine Johnson in 1797. Several diplomatic posts followed until he returned to Boston in 1801.

In 1802 he was elected to the United States Senate as a Federalist. He lost favor with the party because of his stand on such issues as the Louisiana Purchase and the embargo, causing the Federalist Party to demand his resignation and socially ostracize him. In 1809 President Madison rewarded his support of Jefferson by appointing him Minister to Russia.

President Monroe appointed him Secretary of State in 1817. He served with great distinction by negotiating the occupation of Oregon with England, working to obtain Florida from Spain, and forming a close alliance with the President to formulate what would become known as the Monroe Doctrine.

The Secretary of State was considered the political heir to the Presidency in early 19th century American politics. However, the climate was changing and the tradition started giving way to a desire to decide the presidency by popular choice. The Federalist Party had all but dissipated and the Democratic-Republican Party was the one and only political party in existence at the time. However, the party was divided and began separating into a number of different sections and factions. Each section put up its own candidate for the Presidency in 1824. Gen. Andrew Jackson led in both popular and electoral votes. Adams, the candidate of the North, received less votes than Jackson but more than William H. Crawford and Henry Clay. Since no candidate had a majority of electoral votes, the election was decided among the top three by the House of Representatives. Clay, who favored a program similar to that of Adams, threw his crucial support in the House to the New Englander and Adams became the sixth President of the United States.

Upon becoming President, Adams appointed Clay as Secretary of State, sparking charges from Jackson and his angry followers that a "corrupt bargain" had taken place. They immediately began their campaign to wrest the Presidency from Adams in 1828.

Despite facing enormous hostility in Congress, Adams proposed a spectacular national program. He recommended bringing the sections of the Federal Government together with a network of highways and canals, as well as develop and conserve the public domain by using funds from the sale of public lands. He broke ground for the 185-mile Chesapeake and Ohio Canal In 1828.

Adams also urged the United States to take a lead in the development of the arts and sciences through the establishment of a national university, the financing of scientific expeditions, and the erection of an observatory. His critics declared such measures transcended constitutional limitations.

The charges of corruption and public plunder by Jackson's forces during the campaign of 1828 led to Adams defeat. He returned to Massachusetts, expecting to spend the remainder of his life in retirement, but instead was elected to the House of Representatives from the Plymouth district in 1830. He spent the remainder of his life serving as a powerful leader in the House, mostly fighting for civil liberties. He led the fight to force Congress to receive antislavery petitions and fathered the Smithsonian Institution.

On February 21, 1848, he collapsed on the floor of the House from a stroke and was carried to the Speaker's Room. He died two days later. To the end, "Old Man Eloquent" displayed his independent thinking and fought for what he considered right.

Andrew Jackson

Seventh President
1829-1837

Born: March 15, 1767 in
Waxhaw, South Carolina

Died: June 8, 1845 at the
Hermitage near Nashville, Tennessee.

Married to
Rachel Donelson Jackson

Andrew Jackson was born in a backwoods settlement in the Carolinas in 1767. His mother was widowed during her pregnancy with him and died herself when he was only fifteen. Living with relatives and neighbors, he finished school and, at age 17, set out to become a lawyer. He acted as clerk for a lawyer in Salisbury, North Carolina while studying law. He then practiced law for a couple of years in the Carolinas, after which he accepted a job as public prosecutor in Nashville, often having to forge through surrounding wilderness full of hostile Indians.

He married Rachel Donelson Robards, the estranged wife of an abusive husband. Jackson threatened the man's life as a result of insults from the disgruntled man, accusing Jackson of dishonoring Robards' wife. Later, when Robards relocated to Kentucky, it was presumed that he had divorced Rachel. Jackson and Rachel were married for two years when they discovered their marriage was invalid. The truth came to light when the divorce finally did occur, and they reacted by promptly marrying a second time. Despite the circumstances, Jackson married into a very prominent family, and they seemed very much in love during their life together.

Jackson was known to be temperamental and fiercely jealous of his honor. Involved in numerous brawls, he once intervened in an argument between a friend and a Mr. Charles Dickinson. This spurred Mr. Dickinson to later make some provocative and insulting remarks about Jackson and his wife on several occasions, including a statement in the Nashville Review calling him "worthless scoundrel, ... a poltroon and a coward." Jackson challenged the accomplished marksman to a duel, during which Dickinson shot him in the chest before he was able to get off a shot. The bullet lodged inches from his heart. Instead of firing his shot into the air, as was customary, Jackson clutched his chest, then slowly raised his pistol, aimed, and pulled the trigger, fatally wounding Dickinson. The bullet in Jackson's chest could not be removed and never properly healed. The abscesses around the slug caused tremendous discomfort and pain for the remainder of his life, which lasted another 39 years. The stigma, as well as the pain, that resulted from that duel followed him throughout his career.

Jackson prospered sufficiently to buy slaves and to build a mansion, the Hermitage, near Nashville. He was the first man elected from Tennessee to the House of Representatives, and he served briefly in the Senate. He became a national hero as a major general when he defeated the British at New Orleans in the War of 1812.

He campaigned against John Quincy Adams for what he believed to be corruption and public plunder resulting from the election of 1824. A number of state political factions rallied around him and by 1828 enough had joined "Old Hickory" to win numerous state elections and control of the Federal administration in Washington. It was one of the dirtiest campaigns ever waged in American politics. During the campaign, Jackson formed an alliance with Martin van Buren of New York who became one of the principal architects with him in forming one of the two parties that grew out of the Democratic-Republican Party. The Jackson party became the Democratic Party and was opposed by the National Republicans, or Whigs.

More than any of his predecessors, Andrew Jackson was elected President by popular vote. As the seventh President of the United States he sought to act as the direct representative of the common man. Van Buren was named his Secretary of State.

Political bitterness and dirty politics continued throughout the first year of Jackson's administration. Rachel reacted badly to the pressure and animosity targeted at her and her husband. As a result, she suffered from repeated heart pains and eventually died of a heart attack on December 23, 1828.

Jackson attempted to eliminate the Electoral College. He also believed Government duties could be "so plain and simple" that offices should rotate among deserving applicants.

Henry Clay, Daniel Webster, and other Whig leaders proclaimed themselves defenders of popular liberties against what they perceived to be the Jackson takeover. Hostile cartoonists portrayed him as King Andrew, stemming from the fact that, unlike previous Presidents, Jackson did not defer to Congress in policy-making. Instead he used his power of the veto and his position as party leader to assume command.

Another battle ensued over the charter of the Second Bank of the United States. Jackson saw the bank as a government-sponsored private corporation that had become a monopoly. The government used the bank as a repository for all its gold and silver, and the bank's bills were accepted as equivalent to gold for any payments to the government. A Federal Depository or government controlled monetary system did not exist at that time. Jackson's hostilities toward the Second Bank caused it to throw its power against him. Clay and Webster, acting as attorneys for the bank, led the fight for its re-charter in Congress. The military mind of Jackson was determined to kill the bank before it had a chance to kill him. In vetoing the re-charter bill, he accused the Bank of enjoying undue economic privilege. The American electorate agreed. He polled more than 56 percent of the popular vote in 1832, tallying up almost five times as many electoral votes as Clay.

Jackson's Vice President, John C. Calhoun, challenged him by aggressively leading forces that tried to rid themselves of a high protective tariff. When South Carolina commenced to nullify the tariff, Jackson ordered armed forces to Charleston and privately threatened to hang Calhoun. Violence seemed imminent until Clay negotiated a compromise: tariffs were lowered and South Carolina dropped nullification. Differences between Jackson and Calhoun mounted, leading eventually to the resignation of the majority of Jackson's cabinet, including Calhoun. Nothing like this decimation of a president's cabinet had happened before, and it was seen as a constitutional crisis, but Jackson weathered the situation, mainly because Congress was adjourned when the cabinet disintegrated. He had his new cabinet in place (though unratified) by the time Congress reconvened.

Van Buren became Vice President during Jackson's second term, succeeding him to the Presidency when "Old Hickory" retired to the Hermitage. Andrew Jackson radically changed the American party system and methods of electioneering. Many feel his actions left the presidency much stronger than it had been. He strengthened the idea of the United States as a nation, rather than a number of states with an agreement to act in concert. Although the violence he portrayed and the methods he used created strong opposition and many enemies, he was still a highly popular man of his time who never failed to capture the imagination of the masses.

Despite chronic sickness and the constant aggravation and pain from the bullet he carried lodged in his chest for nearly forty years, he lived to the ripe old age of 78, and died peacefully at home on June 8, 1845.

Martin Van Buren

Eighth President
1837-1841

Born: December 5, 1782 in
Columbia, New York

Died: July 24, 1862 in New York

Married to
Hannah Hoes Van Buren

Martin Van Buren was born of Dutch descent on Dec. 5, 1782, the son of a tavern-keeper and farmer in Kinderhook, N.Y. A small man standing a mere 5 feet 6 inches tall, he always stood erect and proud, was highly amiable, and dressed immaculately. He married his cousin, Hannah Hoes, in 1807. He never remarried after she died of tuberculosis in 1819. They had three sons (a fourth died in infancy).

As a young lawyer in 1803, Van Buren became active in New York politics, serving as a state senator and attorney general before being elected to the U.S. Senate in 1820. He established an efficient political organization, which became known as the Albany Regency. He used his strong political power to support William H. Crawford in 1824 and Andrew Jackson in 1828. He led the opposition in the Senate to John Quincy Adams' administration and by 1827 emerged as the principal northern leader for Andrew Jackson. He served briefly as governor of New York (1828–1829) before resigning to accept President Jackson's appointment as his Secretary of State.

Cabinet members recommended by Jackson's Vice President, John C. Calhoun, began to show more support for the Vice President than for President Jackson. This shift in loyalty caused van Buren to emerge as Jackson's most trusted adviser. He was soon on close personal terms with Jackson and played an important part in the Jacksonian program.

Calhoun clearly had his eye on the presidency. The rift in the Cabinet became serious because of Jackson's differences with his Vice President. Van Buren orchestrated a way to avoid the impending standoff by convincing Secretary of War Eaton to join him in resigning, so that Calhoun's supporters would also resign. It worked. Jackson appointed a new Cabinet, and sought again to reward Van Buren by appointing him Minister to Great Britain, but as President of the Senate, Vice President Calhoun cast the deciding vote against the appointment, making a martyr of Van Buren.

In 1832, the "Little Magician," Van Buren, became Vice President. In 1836, he was elected President. His term of office was overshadowed by the Panic of 1837. The 19th century experienced a cyclical economy of either "boom" or "bust." It crashed when van Buren took office, in large part due to Jackson's financial measures. Jackson's destruction of the Second Bank of the United States had removed restrictions upon the inflationary practices of some state banks. For example, wild speculation in land swept the West, based on easy bank credit. In 1836 Jackson sought to end this speculation by issuing a requirement that lands be purchased with hard money, gold or silver. This created a panic that caused hundreds of banks and businesses to fail. Thousands lost their land and by the time van Buren was sworn in, the country was witnessing the worst depression thus far in its history. It would last for five years.

Van Buren, however, attributed it to the over-expansion of credit and reckless business practices. He sought to establish an independent treasury as repository for federal funds instead of creating a new Bank of the United States or placing government funds in state banks. By continuing Jackson's deflationary policies, van Buren's remedy only deepened and prolonged the depression causing him to become one of the few Democratic Presidents to lose to the Whig Party. William Henry Harrison defeated him in 1840.

He sought re-election again in 1844 and was the leading contender for the Democratic nomination until he publicly opposed immediate annexation of Texas. He was against the expansion of slavery and felt that Texas would only add to slave territory and initiate war with Mexico. Subsequently, he was beaten by the Southern delegations at the Baltimore convention, which served to increase his misgivings about the slave power. He worked behind the scenes with anti-slavery Democrats. He joined in the movement that led to the Free-Soil Party and became its candidate for president in 1848, losing again to a Whig, Zachery Taylor. He subsequently returned to the Democratic Party while continuing to object to its pro-Southern policy.

Upon his retirement, he purchased the old Van Ness mansion on the Hudson River and renamed it Lindenwald. In 1852 at the age of 70, he took a trip to Europe where he spent the next ten years and began to write his political memoirs while in Italy. He was the first ex-president to leave the United States. Shortly after he returned home to Lindenwald near Kinderhook, he developed bronchial asthma and died on July 24, 1862.

James K. Polk

Eleventh President
1845-1849

Born: November 2, 1795 in
Mecklenburg County, North Carolina

Died: June 15, 1849 in
Nashville, Tennessee

Married to
Sarah Childress Polk

James K. Polk was born on November 2, 1795 in Mecklenburg County, North Carolina. Studious, industrious, and graduating with honors in 1818 from the University of North Carolina, he became another young lawyer to enter politics. He served in the Tennessee legislature where he became a friend of Andrew Jackson.

He served in the House of Representatives when Jackson was President and was a staunch supporter of Jackson's Bank war. Jackson was such a mentor to the young statesman that Polk was often referred to as "Young Hickory." He served as Speaker between 1835 and 1839, leaving to become Governor of Tennessee following Jackson's advice.

He was a leading contender for the Democratic nomination for Vice President in 1844. Both Martin Van Buren, who had been expected to win the Democratic nomination for President, and Henry Clay, who was certain to be the Whig nominee, declared openly that they opposed the annexation of Texas. This was an effort to take the expansionist issue out of the campaign. However, Polk publicly asserted not only that Texas should be "re-annexed," but also that all of Oregon should be "re-occupied." Polk also favored acquiring California. An elderly Jackson sensed that the populace favored expansion and he urged choosing a candidate committed to the Nation's "Manifest Destiny." When this view prevailed at the Democratic Convention, Polk was nominated on the ninth ballot and became the first "dark horse" President.

The Republic of Texas had gained its independence from Mexico in 1836, but Mexico continued to fight to regain control of the territory. Many Texans supported annexation even before Texas became a sovereign republic. Congress passed a joint resolution to annex Texas before Polk even took office, causing him to face the very real possibility of a war with Mexico. Polk signed the legislation on December 29, 1845 making Texas the 28th state. Ironically, Polk never set foot in Texas.

Oregon was an issue as well. There were extremists who wanted to go even further than Polk in obtaining the Oregon territory, demanding the entire region from the California border to the southern boundary of Alaska (latitude 54'40') crying "Fifty-four forty or fight!" However, Polk realized that any chance of obtaining all of Oregon could only be achieved by going to war with Great Britain. He tried to negotiate a compromise by offering to extend the Canadian boundary along the 49th parallel from the Rocky Mountains to the Pacific Ocean. At first, Britain refused, but when Polk then insisted on the entire region instead, the Brits, wanting to avoid a war as much as the U.S., reversed their position and accepted the 49th parallel proposal. The treaty was signed in 1846.

In his attempt to acquire California and the country of New Mexico, Polk offered Mexico $20 million plus a settlement of damage claims to Americans. General Zachary Taylor was sent to the area on the Rio Grande to bring pressure to the Mexican leadership, when they refused to receive the envoy. Seeing this move as an act of aggression, Mexican troops attacked Taylor's army. Congress declared war. It was 1846 and American forces won repeated victories for the next two years until eventually taking Mexico City. Following the occupation, the Mexicans relinquished New Mexico and California in exchange for $15 million and American assumption of the damage claims.

The United States achieved its greatest territorial expansion under Polk's presidency, extending westward all the way to the Pacific Coast. However, the acquisition of this vast territory gave rise to a bitter quarrel between the North and the South over the expansion of slavery.

Polk had the distinction of delivering all of his campaign promises, but his four years in office were brutal. He died of cholera on June 15, 1849 at the age of 53, just a few months after his presidency ended.

Franklin Pierce

Fourteenth President
1853-1857

Born: November 23, 1804 in
Hillsboro, New Hamphire

Died: October 8, 1869 in
Concord, New Hamphire

Married to
Jane Means Appleton Pierce

Franklin Pierce was born in Hillsboro, New Hampshire, on Nov. 23, 1804. He studied law after graduation from Bowdoin College and entered politics. Elected to the New Hampshire legislature at the age of 24, he became Speaker of the House two years later. He served in the U.S. House of Representatives from 1833 to 1837 and in the U.S. Senate from 1837 to 1842. He married Jane Means Appleton in 1834. His wife loathed the Washington lifestyle so much that Pierce resigned from the Senate in 1842 and began a successful law practice in Concord, New Hampshire.

He served as a brigadier general during the Mexican War. After the war, a group of New Hampshire friends proposed he seek the Presidential nomination in 1852. Delegates at the Democratic convention developed a platform almost immediately. They adopted supporting the Compromise of 1850, which dealt with land issues and slavery of the vast territory acquired during Polk's administration. However, they had a difficult time deciding on a nominee and by the end of the 48th ballot had eliminated all of the well-known candidates and settled on Pierce as a "dark horse." Polk became the Democratic candidate for President on the 49th ballot.

He defeated the Whig candidate, Gen. Winfield Scott, by a narrow margin of popular votes, probably because the Democrats stood more firmly behind the Compromise and Scott, who had been his commander during the Mexican War, was not trusted in the South.

Two months before he took office, he and his wife witnessed the death of their eleven-year-old son in a train wreck. Pierce entered the Presidency grief-stricken, nervous, and exhausted. His term began with a sense of national tranquility despite his personal anxieties, but that soon changed when he started implementing his policies. When he pressured Great Britain to relinquish its special interests along part of the Central American coast and tried to persuade Spain to sell Cuba, he angered northerners who were convinced his efforts intended to extend slavery into other areas. He tried to annex Hawaii, acquire a naval base in Santo Domingo, and purchase Alaska, all of which were unsuccessful.

His biggest backlash came from backing Stephan Douglas' proposed Kansas-Nebraska Act, which repealed the Missouri Compromise and reopened the question of slavery in the West. Pierce was interested in establishing a railroad from Chicago to California through Nebraska. He had already sent James Gadsen to Mexico on the advice of his Secretary of War, Jefferson Davis, to purchase additional land for $10 million in what is now southern Arizona and part of southern New Mexico in order to lay track for a southern railroad route. All of his plans for a transcontinental railroad would be unsuccessful. However, the Douglas proposal caused a lot of trouble by suggesting that residents in the new territories be allowed to decide for themselves the issue of slavery. As a result, an influx of both southerners and northerners rushed into Kansas to vie for control of the territory. Shooting broke out. "Bleeding Kansas" became a prelude to the Civil War.

By the end of his administration, Pierce had become highly unpopular and, as a result, failed to gain the Democratic nomination for re-election. The Democrats turned instead to the less controversial James Buchanan. Pierce returned to New Hampshire, where he died in relative obscurity in Concord on October 8, 1869.

James Buchanan

Fifteenth President
1857-1861

Born: April 23, 1791 in Cove Gap
near Mercersburg, Pennsylvania

Died: June 1, 1868 in
Lancaster, Pennsylvania

Never married, was
Harriet Lane's uncle

James Buchanan was born in a log house at Stony Batter in Cove Gap, Pennsylvania on April 23, 1791. He was the eldest of 11 children of a well-to-do family of Scotch-Irish immigrants, his father being a successful storekeeper and landowner. He graduated from Dickinson College with a law degree and became a gifted debater. He was admitted to the Bar in 1812, moving to Lancaster to set up practice.

He was engaged to be married when he was 28, but his fiancée broke off their engagement following a misunderstanding. Before he could resolve the dispute and reconcile their differences, she died. Buchanan never got over the tragedy and remained unmarried for the duration of his life, becoming the first (and, to date, only) bachelor President.

He was elected to the Pennsylvania House of Representatives in 1814 and to the United States House of Representatives in 1821, where he served five terms. President Andrew Jackson appointed him as the Minister to Russia in 1832, where he negotiated the first-ever commercial treaty with that country. After his return in 1834, he served in the United States Senate for a decade until President James K. Polk appointed him Secretary of State in 1845. He then served as Minister to Great Britain under President Franklin Pierce.

His service abroad probably contributed heavily to his receiving the Democratic nomination for President in 1856, because it isolated him from the controversies stemming from Pierce's administration. Even though he had sought the nomination unsuccessfully three times before, by 1856 he had grown weary of public service and was ready to retire. He accepted the nomination strictly out of a sense of duty and the obligation he felt to the country and his party. Therefore, the tall, stately, stiffly formal statesman opted to remain quietly at his home in Wheatland instead of actively campaigning for the nation's top position.

Buchanan naively believed the slave issue was about to dissipate and that the crisis would disappear altogether if he could maintain a sectional balance in his appointments. He was convinced that the Supreme Court was about to bring the dispute to a close and that the nation would accept constitutional law as the Supreme Court interpreted it. Therefore, he announced in his Inaugural Address that the question was of "little practical importance" and that the Supreme Court was about to "speedily and finally" settle it.

Two days later Chief Justice Roger B. Taney rendered the Dred Scott decision. The Supreme Court decision declared that Congress had no constitutional power to deprive persons of their property rights in slaves in the territories. The decision met with widespread approval in the South, but created turbulence in the North. Buchanan did not sense the pulse of the political realities of the time.

He understood the nation was divided, but failed to recognize just how divisive it was becoming. It realigned political parties. The Democrats split and the Whigs disintegrated, causing the emergence of a whole new faction, the Republican Party.

In an attempt to end the controversy in Kansas, he advocated admitting the territory as a slave state. His actions angered the Republicans even more and alienated members of his own party. Kansas remained a territory. Then Republicans won a plurality in the House in 1858. Every significant bill they passed either fell through before southern votes in the Senate or became victim to Presidential veto. The Federal Government reached a stalemate.

As the election of 1860 approached, the Democratic Party split into northern and southern wings, each nominating its own candidate for the Presidency. This meant that the unknown Republican candidate, Abraham Lincoln, would likely get elected even though his name didn't appear on any southern ballot. Rather than accept a Republican administration, the southern proslavery extremists referred to as "fire-eaters" advocated seceding from the Union and forming their own Southern government. President Buchanan refused to allow states to secede but admitted that the Federal Government legally could not prevent them. He tried in vain to reach a compromise, but secessionist leaders did not want compromise.

The seceding states failed to seize federal forts in Florida and South Carolina. Buchanan sent the Star of the West to carry reinforcements to Fort Sumter in January 1861, but the mission was never completed and the ship returned to New York. Buchanan never considered surrendering the forts to the South, but he returned to his previous policy of maintaining the status quo when the steamship failed to deliver its human cargo. An unofficial truce prevailed at the garrisons. They remained in federal hands at the end of his presidency, but the forts were more difficult to defend because they never received reinforcements, a problem Buchanan left to the responsibility of his successor.

On March 4, 1861, a weary and relieved Buchanan left office and retired to his Wheatland estate. He died on June 1, 1868, at the age of seventy-seven, from a severe cold and the complications of old age.

Andrew Johnson

Seventeenth President
1865-1869

Born: December 29, 1808 in
Raleigh, North Carolina

Died: July 31, 1875 in
Carter's Station, Tennessee

Married to
Eliza McArdle Johns

Andrew Johnson was born in Raleigh, North Carolina on Dec. 29, 1808, the younger of two sons of working class parents. Andrew's father died when he was four. His mother apprenticed him and his brother to a local tailor when he was 14 to help them learn a trade. He never attended school, but received informal training through his apprenticeship and taught himself to read. An act of mischief forced him to run away. Years later, he returned home to his mother, brother and stepfather and, due to a lack of employment opportunities, led his family to Greeneville, Tennessee, where he opened a tailor shop. There he met Eliza McCardle, whom he married on May 17, 1827. Eliza was an educated woman and worked with her husband to improve his reading and writing skills. She also taught him arithmetic. Johnson's business improved as a result and his shop soon became a gathering place for political discussions. He joined a debate club at a nearby small college. The encouragement from his wife, coupled with the speaking skills he developed both in his shop and at his debate club, steered Johnson into politics.

His first election made him an alderman of Greeneville, Tennessee in 1828. Two years later he became mayor. He was elected to the Tennessee House of Representatives in 1835 and again in 1839. Following his second term, he ran successfully for a seat in the Tennessee Senate. He was a representative for the common man, supporting rights of free laborers and attempting to repeal a law beneficial to slaveholders. He also unsuccessfully attempted to create a new state called Frankland from the Appalachian regions of North Carolina, Virginia, Georgia, and Tennessee.

He was elected to the U.S. House of Representatives in 1843, retaining his seat until 1853. While there, he supported President Polk's handling of the Texas annexation, Oregon acquisition, and Mexican War. He advocated a homestead bill to provide a free farm for the poor man. Unlike most of his Southern compatriots, he supported the Constitution over State's Rights. He left the legislature when he won the Tennessee gubernatorial election that year and was re-elected in 1855. As governor, Johnson established a public school system and a state library in Tennessee. On the eve of the Civil War in 1857, he was elected to the U.S. Senate, where he remained even when Tennessee seceded. This act made him a hero in the North and a traitor in the minds of most Southerners. In 1862 President Lincoln appointed him Military Governor of Tennessee, and Johnson used the state as a laboratory for reconstruction. In 1864 the Republicans, contending that their National Union Party was for all loyal men, nominated the Southern Democrat Johnson for Vice President.

Johnson took the oath of office in March 1865. The following month a conspiracy to assassinate key members of the government, including the President and Vice President, was carried out. President Lincoln went to

Ford's Theater in Washington for an evening of entertainment and was assassinated by John Wilkes Booth. The assassin designated to kill the vice-president lost heart and did not attempt the assassination. Johnson became president on April 15, 1865.

The Presidency fell upon an old-fashioned southern Jacksonian Democrat who was unprepared to meet the Radical Republican congressional opposition he faced. His top priority was reconstruction. Johnson immediately set out to reconstruct the former Confederate States while Congress was not in session. He was willing to pardon all who would take an oath of allegiance, but required leaders and men of wealth to obtain special Presidential pardons. By the time Congress met in December, most southern states had been reconstructed and slavery was being abolished, despite "black codes" designed to regulate the emancipation by imposing prewar restrictions upon Negroes.

The Radical Republicans in Congress created a strong united front to reverse Johnson's program. Their first move was to refuse to seat any Senator or Representative from the old Confederacy. They also passed legislation dealing with former slaves. Johnson vetoed the measures, but the Radicals gathered enough votes to override his veto. This marked the first time that Congress had overridden a Presidential veto on an important bill. The Civil Rights Act of 1866 passed, establishing Negroes as American citizens forbidding discrimination against them.

A few months later Congress submitted to the states the Fourteenth Amendment, specifying that no state should "deprive any person of life, liberty, or property, without due process of law." Tennessee was the only former Confederate State willing to ratify the amendment. Two bloody race riots broke out in the South.

Radical Republicans won an overwhelming victory in Congress during the fall elections. In March 1867, the Radicals enacted their own plan of Reconstruction, which again placed southern states under military rule. They passed laws placing restrictions upon the President. When Johnson dismissed Secretary of War Edwin M. Stanton, he was accused of violating the Tenure of Office Act. The House voted eleven articles of impeachment against him. He was tried by the Senate in the spring of 1868 and acquitted by one vote.

Andrew Johnson completed the remainder of Abraham Lincoln's term of office but failed to receive his party's nomination in 1869. He returned to Greeneville, Tennessee, where he remained active in politics. In 1875 he returned to public service when he was elected to the U.S. Senate. Later that same year, Andrew Johnson suffered a stroke and died on July 31 near Carter Station, Tennessee. He was laid to rest in a plot on his property in Greeneville with his request fulfilled of being buried wrapped in an American flag and placed on a copy of the Constitution.

Grover Cleveland

Twenty-Second President
1885-1889
Twenty-Fourth President
1893-1897

Born: March 18, 1837 in
Caldwell, New Jersey

Died: June 24, 1908 in his home in
Princeton New Jersey

Married to
Frances Folsom Cleveland

Stephen Grover Cleveland was born on March 18, 1837, in Caldwell, New Jersey, the fifth of nine children. His father, the Reverend Richard Falley Cleveland, was minister of the Caldwell Presbyterian Church. From the time Grover was 4 until he was 13, the family lived in Fayetteville, New York.

The chubby young boy could out swim and out wrestle most of the boys his age and he loved to fish, a favorite pastime that remained with him throughout his life. The family moved to Clinton, New York in 1850. After his father died suddenly when Grover was 16, his uncle helped him get a job as a law clerk in a Buffalo law office. Within 10 years he was admitted to the bar and made assistant district attorney for Erie County. Honesty and a sense of fair play in the district attorney's office led to him being elected Sheriff and in 1881 he went on to become mayor of Buffalo. He developed a political track record of ruthless honesty and of cleaning up corruption everywhere he went, causing reform Democrats to nominate him for the top political position in the state. In 1881, he became Governor of the State of New York.

His reputation for honesty and for fighting corruption made him the perfect choice as the Democrats' presidential candidate in 1884. He was clearly placed on the ballot because of the number of scandals that plagued Washington, D.C. at the time. So powerful was his reputation, that his nomination at the Democratic National Convention was seconded with a delegate proclaiming, "We love him most for the enemies he has made."

The campaign was dirty and close, but Grover Cleveland became the 22nd President of the United States and the first Democrat to be elected since James Buchanan in 1857 (Andrew Johnson, a Democrat, assumed the Presidency when Lincoln died, but was not re-elected). Single when he entered the office, Cleveland married Frances Folsom, 28 years his junior, in 1886 to become the only President to date to be married in the White House.

He vetoed several bills during his first term, such as a seed grain distribution bill for drought-stricken farmers in Texas, a number of private pension bills to Civil War veterans, and a bill granting pensions for disabilities not caused by military service. He set a policy to bar special favors to economic groups and signed the Interstate Commerce Act, the first federal attempt to regulate the railroads. When he asked Congress to reduce high protective tariffs in late 1887, he pretty much sealed his fate the following election year. Although he won a larger popular majority in 1888, his opponent, Benjamin Harrison, won the majority of the electoral votes. However, Cleveland ran again during the next election and was elected the 24th President of the United States in 1892, becoming the only President to serve two non-consecutive terms.

During this tenure, he faced a depression causing widespread business failures, farm mortgage foreclosures, and unemployment. He attempted to reverse the economic failure by repealing the Sherman Silver Purchase Act. With the aid of Wall Street, he managed to maintain the Treasury's gold reserve. He sent Federal troops to enforce an injunction against striking railroad workers in Chicago and forced Great Britain to accept arbitration of a Venezuela boundary dispute. No one ever argued that Grover Cleveland always did what he believed was the honest thing to do, but his actions still angered some powerful groups in his own party. For the most part, his policies during the depression were unpopular and the party responded by nominating William Jennings Bryan as the Democratic candidate in 1896.

He left the White House for the last time in January 1897, retiring from politics, to live the remainder of his life in Princeton, New Jersey. He died on June 24, 1908.

Woodrow Wilson

Twenty-Eighth President
1913-1921

Born: December 28, 1856 in
Staunton, Virginia

Died: February 3, 1924 in
Washington, D.C.

Married to Ellen Louise Axson
Wilson and to
Edith Bolling Galt Wilson

Thomas Woodrow Wilson was born in Staunton, Virginia, on December 29, 1856 (because he was born around midnight, he always claimed his birthday was December 28). The son of a Presbyterian minister, he was one of four children with two older sisters and a younger brother.

He was close to his father, Joseph, who was also his mentor, teacher, frequent companion, and friend. He attended private schools until he qualified for admission to North Carolina's Davidson College in 1873. At the end of his freshman year he left Davidson and enrolled at the College of New Jersey (now Princeton University). He graduated from Princeton and in 1879 entered the University of Virginia to study law. He started a law practice in Atlanta, where he met Ellen Louise Axson, whose father shared his father's vocation as a Presbyterian minister. Following an unsuccessful year as an attorney in Atlanta, he returned to academics by entering Johns Hopkins University in Baltimore to receive his doctorate and prepare for a teaching career.

He and Ellen were married in 1885 and they made their home in Bryn Mawr, Pennsylvania, where he began his teaching career as an associate professor at the new Bryn Mawr College. They had three daughters.

In 1888, Wilson accepted a professorship at Wesleyan University in Connecticut, where, in addition to teaching, he also coached football. He published a textbook on modern government in 1889 entitled *The State*, and authored a number of subsequent books, such as *Division and Reunion*, a history of the United States between the Andrew Jackson era and Reconstruction and a five-volume *History of the American People*. His growing reputation as a scholar led him to become professor of law at Princeton University in 1890. He advanced rapidly as a professor of political science and became president of Princeton in 1902. A dispute materialized between Wilson and the dean of the graduate school over the site of a new graduate college that became a battle for control of the university itself. The clash between the two almost destroyed the university. The conflict was decided when a wealthy alumni died leaving a substantial bequeath to build the new graduate school and naming Wilson's adversary as trustee.

Wilson's growing national reputation had for years prompted some conservative Democrats to try to get him to enter politics. They offered to back him for political office in New Jersey. When his plans at Princeton were defeated, he decided to accept their offer and ran successfully for Governor in 1910, endorsing a progressive platform and asserting his independence of the very machine that had nominated him.

He immediately set out to establish a wide range of reforms. He helped create a system of direct primary elections, in which the voters nominated the party candidates; a public service commission with power over the services and charges of public utilities and railroads; and an insurance system to help injured workers.

His progressive measures as governor of New Jersey gained Wilson a lot of publicity. He became a national figure and a leading candidate for the Democratic presidential nomination in 1912. The struggle for the nomination at the Democratic National Convention in Baltimore was a long and heated one, but Wilson eventually won the choice of his party on the 46th ballot.

Campaigning on a program stressing individualism and states' rights called the New Freedom, he won the election despite receiving only 42 percent of the popular vote with an overwhelming number of electoral votes in a three-way election.

Several pertinent pieces of legislation were passed during the Wilson administration: the Underwood Act, which lowered tariffs containing a graduated Federal income tax measure; the Federal Reserve Act; antitrust legislation establishing a Federal Trade Commission; a child labor law; and legislation limiting the work day to eight hours for railroad workers. These bills, coupled with the slogan "He kept us out of war" served to re-elect him. However, within weeks of the inauguration of his second term, it became evident that America could not remain neutral in the World War and on April 2, 1917 President Wilson asked Congress to declare war on Germany.

The following year, he proposed establishing "a general association of nations." Following the Armistice with Germany in November 1918, he presented the Versailles Treaty to the Senate, in which the Covenant of the League of Nations appeared, but the Republican majority Congress wanted to change America's obligations outlined in the treaty. Against doctors' advice, Wilson embarked on a lengthy speaking tour to gain public support for the treaty and suffered a stroke that paralyzed him on one side. Despite his efforts, the Senate failed to ratify the treaty. The Warren Harding landslide of 1920 pretty much assured that the United States would not become a member of the League of Nations, even though Wilson received the Nobel Peace Prize that same year for his efforts in establishing the organization.

Woodrow Wilson left the White House in 1921 and retired to his home in Washington, D.C. He was convinced that someday the American people would embrace his vision of a united world working together for peace and progress. He died on February 3, 1924, and is buried in the National Cathedral in Washington.

Franklin D. Roosevelt

Thirty-Second President
1933-1945

Born: January 30, 1882 in
Hyde Park, New York

Died: April 12, 1945 in
Warm Springs, Georgia

Married to
Anna Eleanor Roosevelt

Franklin Roosevelt was born to wealthy parents at Hyde Park, New York overlooking the Hudson River, on January 30, 1882. His father was a well-to-do investor and vice president of a small railroad, while his mother came from a wealthy New England family.

He graduated from Harvard University in 1904, where he served as chief editor of the student newspaper, Crimson, and went to Columbia University Law School. He married his distant cousin, Eleanor Roosevelt, on St. Patrick's Day in 1905. President Theodore Roosevelt, Franklin's fifth cousin and Eleanor's uncle, gave her in marriage.

Franklin greatly admired his distant cousin, Teddy, and wanted to follow in his footsteps of politics and public service, but as a Democrat. He went to work briefly for a Wall Street law firm before Democratic leaders in Dutchess County, New York persuaded him to run for a Senate seat in 1910 that seemed impossible for the party to fill. The young Roosevelt ran an energetic campaign and, when the Republicans split their vote, he emerged victorious and won his first election. He was appointed President Wilson's Assistant Secretary of the Navy, and became the Democratic nominee for Vice President in 1920 during the Republican landslide that elected Warren G. Harding.

Roosevelt entered the private sector while maintaining his interest in politics. During a vacation at Campobello Island in Canada in the summer of 1921, the 39-year-old politician was suddenly stricken with poliomyelitis. Eleanor refused to let him feel as though his political career was over. The mother of their five children kept his aspirations alive, often by appearing for her husband at political meetings, and encouraging him to pursue his political career. Roosevelt fought hard to regain the use of his legs through exercise and swimming. He needed leg braces, a cane, and a strong arm on which to lean, but in spite of his infliction with polio he remained one of the dominant figures in the Democratic Party. At the 1924 Democratic National Convention he made a dramatic appearance on crutches to nominate Alfred E. Smith for President.

In 1928 he was elected Governor of New York. His re-election in 1930 by a record majority made him the leading candidate for President on the 1932 Democratic ticket. The Great Depression plagued the country and was the only issue that mattered to the American people in this campaign. Roosevelt's promise of a "New Deal" unseated Herbert Hoover's bid for re-election by more than 7 million popular votes and a margin of 472 to 59 electoral votes.

The 20th Amendment to the Constitution, changing the presidential inauguration date to January 20, did not go into effect until October 1933. This was significant because Roosevelt's inauguration didn't take place until March 4, 1933. By that time, the Depression had turned the economy upside down. Depositors became afraid of losing their savings and began withdrawing their money in droves. This sudden run on the banks caused thousands of the financial institutions to collapse. Twenty-five percent of the nation's wage earners, some 13 million individuals, were unemployed. Low prices on basic crops were causing farmers to lose their farms and food became scarce. The country was in the worst economic crisis in its history.

The first thing Roosevelt did was to close all U.S. banks to prevent further collapse and call Congress into special session to pass emergency banking legislation. The Federal Deposit Insurance Corporation was established to insure bank deposits and protect people from losing their savings. Within a few days most banks were reopened, and money that had been withdrawn was being re-deposited.

During his first hundred days, Roosevelt proposed his New Deal reforms to provide relief to the needy and recovery to the economy. During his first two terms in office, a wide variety of legislation was approved by Congress and designed to bring recovery to business and agriculture, give relief to the unemployed, and help to landowners threatened with losing their farms and homes. The Tennessee Valley Authority (TVA) was created to provide flood control, cheap electricity, and better use of the land for the entire poverty-stricken Tennessee River area; a federal agency provided states with funds to feed the hungry; aid was given to farmers and homeowners in danger of losing their property by not being able to keep up mortgage payments; the Agricultural Adjustment Administration (AAA) limited production of basic crops and livestock in order to raise prices and thus increase farmers' incomes; and the National Recovery Administration (NRA) established codes of fair competition in major industries for which businesses were expected to pay at least minimum wages and to work their employees for no more than established maximum hours. The NRA also gave workers the right to bargain collectively, provisions that were replaced by the National Labor Relations Act of 1935, which gave strong protection to unions and encouraged the growth of the labor movement.

At the president's urging, Congress took the United States off the gold standard and devaluated the dollar. This lowered its exchange value, allowing American products to be sold to better advantage abroad.

A certain measure of recovery was realized by 1935, but an increasing number of businessmen and bankers were turning against Roosevelt's New Deal program. Their biggest concerns were being taken off the gold standard, deficit in the budget, and the concessions given to labor. He responded by creating the Social Security program, imposing heavier taxes on the wealthy, developing new controls over banks and public utilities, and establishing The Civilian Conservation Corps (CCC), an enormous work relief program that provided jobs in forest conservation and road construction work for the unemployed. The U.S. Supreme Court declared the NRA code system unconstitutional and ruled against part of the AAA. Still, the economy showed a remarkable recovery.

In 1936 he was re-elected to a second term by a vast margin. Interpreting this landslide as an overwhelming approval of his New Deal, Roosevelt set out to negate the Supreme Court's impact on the program by petitioning to expand the Court by six members. The effort failed and brought unexpected criticism to the popular president. By 1937 the economy had almost reached the prosperity levels of the 1920s, although unemployment continued to be high. When Roosevelt cut New Deal spending in an effort to balance the federal budget, a sharp recession followed. He returned to heavy spending, and the trend toward recovery resumed.

France and England declared war against Germany and the Nazi regime of Adolf Hitler following German occupation of Austria in 1938, Czechoslovakia and Poland in 1939.

Elected to a third term in 1940, Roosevelt pledged the United States to a "good neighbor" policy, transforming the Monroe Doctrine from a unilateral American manifesto into arrangements for mutual action against aggressors. While doing all he could to help strengthen nations being threatened or attacked, he also did everything in his power to keep the United States out of the war in Europe. When France fell and England came under siege in 1940, he sent all possible aid short of actual military involvement to Great Britain.

Then the Japanese attacked Pearl Harbor on December 7, 1941. Roosevelt declared war on Japan and directed organization of the Nation's manpower and resources for global war.

Roosevelt was elected to an unprecedented fourth term in 1944. Because he felt that the future peace of the world depended upon relations between the two great superpowers of the United States and Russia, he spent almost as much time thinking about the planning of a United Nations to be able to settle international disputes to avoid war as he did thinking about the war effort. As the war drew to a close, Roosevelt's health deteriorated. In an effort to rest and recover from a grueling campaign, he took time off to rest at his home in Warm Springs, Georgia. He died of a cerebral hemorrhage on April 12, 1945, less than a month before the war in Europe came to an end, leaving the remainder of his fourth term in the hands of his Vice President Harry S. Truman.

Harry S. Truman

Thirty-Third President
1945-1953

Born: May 8, 1884 in
Lamar, Missouri

Died: December 26, 1972 in
Independence, Missouri

Married to
Elizabeth Virginia Wallace Truman

Harry S. Truman was born in Lamar, Missouri, on May 8, 1884, the eldest of three children. His parents gave young Harry the letter "S" instead of a middle name because they couldn't decide which of his grandfathers to name him after.

He grew up in Independence, Missouri. His father couldn't afford to send him to college, so after high school, Harry held a number of jobs, eventually becoming a bank clerk. At the age of 22 in 1906, he went to work on the family farm, where he prospered for the next 11 years.

He served in the First World War as an officer with a field artillery unit in France, reaching the rank of captain. When he returned home after the war in 1919, he married his childhood sweetheart, Elizabeth "Bess" Virginia Wallace and opened a men's clothing store in Kansas City.

At the urging of his friends, he entered politics as a Democrat with strong views, just like his father. In 1922, he was elected to the Jackson County Court. Despite the fact that his duties were administrative rather than judicial, his friends and acquaintances called him Judge Truman. Still, he felt his new responsibilities required he have knowledge of law, so he studied at night for two years at the Kansas City School of Law. In 1926 he was elected presiding judge, an office he held for almost nine years. In 1934 he was elected to the United States Senate and was re-elected in 1940.

Truman, concerned that Missouri was not getting its fair share of defense contracts and bothered by reports of inefficient waste and corruption in the defense program, proposed a Senate investigation of the national defense program. The Senate War Investigating Committee was formed with Truman as chairman. The committee, better known as the Truman Committee, became the political watchdog of the Roosevelt Administration during World War II and uncovered widespread corruption and waste, saving the government as much as $15 billion in the process.

The success of the committee and his support of Roosevelt's policies led Truman's political supporters to back him for the Democratic nomination for vice president in the election of 1944 in President Roosevelt's run for a fourth term. They were elected easily. Truman held the office for just 12 weeks. President Roosevelt suddenly died on April 12, 1945, forcing Truman to inherit a host of wartime problems without any briefings. He once confessed to reporters, "I felt like the moon, the stars, and all the planets had fallen on me."

The new president had to make some of the most crucial decisions in world history. When Japan rejected a plea to surrender, Truman ordered atomic bombs to be dropped on Hiroshima and Nagasaki, Japanese cities devoted to war work. Japan quickly surrendered.

Truman saw Presidents Wilson and Roosevelt's dreams come true when he witnessed the signing of the charter of the United Nations in June 1945. For the most part in the beginning, he followed his predecessor's policies, but it wasn't long before he began developing his own. He presented a 21-point program to Congress. What became known as the Fair Deal proposed the expansion of Social Security, a full-employment program, a permanent Fair Employment Practices Act, and public housing and slum clearance.

Truman excelled in foreign affairs. He persuaded Congress to launch the Truman Doctrine, which aided Turkey and Greece, two countries being pressured and threatened by a Soviet Union takeover. The Marshall Plan, named for his Secretary of State, stimulated amazing economic recovery in war-torn Western Europe. He created the Berlin airlift to supply Berliners when Russia blockaded the western sectors of the city in 1948 and kept the airlift going until the Russians backed down. At the same time, he campaigned successfully to be re-elected then negotiated the North Atlantic Treaty Organization as a military alliance to protect Western nations. NATO was established in 1949.

In June 1950, the Communist government of North Korea attacked South Korea. The skirmish was technically what Truman called "a police action by the United Nations," but turned into a long, hopeless struggle as U.N. forces held a line above the old boundary of South Korea. Truman wanted to keep the war limited and avoid a major conflict with China and perhaps Russia at all costs. When the popular and high profile United Nations commander, U.S. General Douglas MacArthur, proposed bombing bases in China, Truman refused to give the order, fearing that it would result in all-out war. MacArthur turned to Republicans in Congress in an effort to get Truman's orders reversed and the President promptly relieved the General of his command. The Korean conflict did not come to an end until the armistice was reached in July 1953, after Truman left office.

Opting not to seek re-election, Truman left office in January 1953 and retired to his home in Independence, Missouri. He traveled, published his memoirs, and enjoyed the status of an elder statesman until he died on December 26, 1972.

John F. Kennedy

Thirty-Fifth President
1961-1963

Born: May 29, 1917 in
Bookline, Massachusetts

Died: November 22, 1963. Killed by
an assassin's bullet in Dallas, Texas

Married to
Jacqueline Lee Bouvier Kennedy

John Fitzgerald Kennedy was born on May 29, 1917, on the outskirts of Boston in Brookline, Massachusetts. He was the second of nine children in a wealthy Irish Catholic family with a long and powerful political tradition. His father, Joseph Patrick Kennedy, was a self-made multi-millionaire active in politics who built a financial empire, served as Ambassador to England, and married the daughter of Boston mayor "Honey Fitz" Fitzgerald.

Like his father before him, "Jack" graduated from Harvard University. In 1940, young Kennedy was commissioned into the U.S. Navy to serve as commander of the torpedo boat PT-109 in the South Pacific. One night, while on a routine patrol, the PT boat was struck by a Japanese destroyer, broke in half and sank. Kennedy, athletic and an excellent swimmer, heroically took control and guided his men three miles in the dark through perilous waters to an island, towing an injured sailor to safety, despite suffering a back injury, using his teeth to pull the man by his vest straps. Once on the island, he and a fellow officer swam back and forth to other islands seeking help. Finding a couple of natives in a canoe, Kennedy scratched a message on a coconut for the natives to take to a U.S. naval base. The crew was rescued five days later and Kennedy received the Navy and Marine Corps Medal for his courage and leadership. His back injury forced him to accept a medical discharge in 1945.

Back in Boston, he successfully ran for the U.S. House of Representatives as the Democratic candidate in 1946 and was twice re-elected. In 1952 he was elected to the U.S. Senate. The following year he married Jacqueline Bouvier. They had three children, although the youngest, Patrick, died in infancy.

Having established a reputation as a liberal in Congress, he was criticized for not taking a firm stand against Joseph McCarthy in the early 1950s. He was in the hospital for back surgery on December 2, 1954 when the Senate voted to reprimand the Wisconsin Republican for his methods and scare tactics in investigating the spread of Communism in America. While recuperating from the operation, Kennedy wrote *Profiles in Courage*, which won the Pulitzer Prize in history in 1957.

He gained widespread public attention due to television coverage at the National Democratic Convention in Chicago in 1956 when he missed being placed on the ballot as Vice President by just a few votes. This recognition allowed him to receive the nomination for President on the first ballot four years later. Kennedy recognized that being a Northerner and Roman Catholic were obstacles to winning Southern votes and shrewdly chose Lyndon B. Johnson of Texas as his running mate. Millions viewed the televised debates between him and the Republican nominee, Richard M. Nixon. Kennedy came across well on television and many experts agree that his charm and public appeal, more than his stand on issues, led to his winning the election by a narrow margin in the popular vote.

The major issues facing his presidency were the Cold War with the Soviet Union, civil rights, and unemployment. Almost immediately after taking office, he had two dangerous confrontations with the Soviets. The Russians built the Berlin Wall to separate Communist-controlled East Berlin from allied-backed West Berlin to which Kennedy responded by increasing U.S. military forces in the region. The Soviet threat subsided by 1962, but flared up again in Cuba when satellite photos showed the presence of Soviet missiles and military troops on the island. Kennedy demanded their removal, and when the Soviets refused, he initiated a naval blockade of Cuba until Soviet premier Nikita Khrushchev backed down and withdrew.

Relations with the Soviets improved, but the Cold War continued, especially in South Viet Nam compelling Kennedy to increase the number of military advisers in Southeast Asia. He established the Peace Corps and formed the Alliance for Progress in 1961 to provide aid and elicit cooperation between the United States and Latin America in an effort to counter Communist influence in the region. In 1963 the United States and Soviet Union signed a treaty to ban nuclear arms testing in the atmosphere.

The civil rights issue at home was even more challenging. Blacks demonstrated in the South to end segregation. Kennedy had to declare a moral crisis and initiated legislation to provide equal rights for all. Rioting broke out in 1962 when James Meredith, a black student, enrolled at the University of Mississippi. Kennedy sent out the National Guard and federal marshals to the campus to restore order, creating an anti-Kennedy backlash among whites in the South.

Kennedy was committed to getting the country moving again as promised in his inaugural address by insisting that Americans "Ask not what your country can do for you, ask what you can do for your country." His economic programs brought new hope to a nation that once again envisioned prosperity and vitality constantly compared to Camelot. He laid out plans for a massive assault on areas of economic hardship and poverty. He believed that space exploration was the new frontier to unlock answers and technological advancements for the future and was committed to putting a man on the moon by the end of the decade.

On November 22, 1963, John F. Kennedy was assassinated during a motorcade ride through Dallas, Texas. He was buried with full military honors in Arlington Cemetery, a torch embracing an eternal flame to mark his gravesite. John Kennedy was the youngest man to be elected President and the youngest to die.

Lyndon B. Johnson

Thirty-Sixth President
1963-1969

Born: August 27, 1908 near
Stonewall, Texas

Died: January 22, 1973 in
Johnson City, Texas

Married to
Claudia Taylor (Lady Bird) Johnson

Lyndon Johnson was born on August 27, 1908, on a farm near Stonewall, Texas. The family farm was located near Johnson City, a town named after his paternal grandfather and his grandfather's brother. His father was a farmer and cattle investor of modest means, who served five terms in the Texas legislature. Lyndon was the eldest of five children, growing up with three sisters and a brother.

After high school Lyndon went to California to find a direction for his life. After a number of menial jobs washing dishes, waiting tables, and doing farm work, he got homesick and hitchhiked his way back to Texas. After a short period working on a construction crew, he told his parents he wanted to learn to work with his head instead of his hands, borrowed $75 for tuition, and enrolled at Southwest Texas State Teachers College in San Marcos, where he majored in history. He took on several jobs to help pay his way through college. He was vigorous in his pursuit of an education. He led the debating team, edited the college newspaper, and was a member of the literary society. He graduated with a Bachelor of Science degree in 1930.

After college, he became a public school teacher in Houston for a brief time. Fascinated by politics, he decided to follow his family's tradition of political involvement and gave up teaching to serve as secretary to a newly elected congressman and family friend in 1931.

He married a girl known as Lady Bird since childhood, Claudia Alta Taylor, of Marshall, Texas, in 1934. They had two daughters, Lynda Bird and Luci Baines.

Another family friend, Congressman Sam Rayburn, who became U.S. Speaker of the House, helped get Lyndon appointed the Texas state director of the National Youth Administration (NYA) in 1935. After two years, Johnson resigned to become a candidate for Congress. He campaigned vigorously in support of FDR's New Deal and won a seat, by a substantial margin, in the U.S. House of Representatives to which he was re-elected five times.

A member of the Naval Reserve when the United States declared war on Japan, he requested active duty and was the first member of the House of Representatives to go into uniform. Seven months later, Roosevelt ordered all members of Congress in military service back to their posts in Washington. Johnson, a lieutenant commander assigned to the Pacific Theater of Operations, was awarded the Silver Star.

He was elected to the U.S. Senate in 1948 and rose quickly to a position of leadership. In 1953 he became the youngest Minority Leader in Senate history. The following year Democrats won control and he became Majority Leader. He was Texas' "favorite son" candidate for President in 1958, but it was not until 1960 that he made a serious bid for nomination when John F. Kennedy asked him to serve as his running mate. As Vice President in line for the presidency on November 22, 1963 when Kennedy was assassinated, Johnson became the 36th President of the United States.

From the outset, he worked to enact legislation Kennedy was trying to pass, most notably a new civil rights bill and a tax cut. He called for an investigation of the Kennedy assassination to be headed up by Chief Justice Earl Warren. The Warren Commission concluded that the assassin, Lee Harvey Oswald, acted alone, although the controversy surrounding a conspiracy continues.

The American public returned Johnson to the White House in 1964 with an unprecedented 61% of the vote and the widest popular margin in American history, totaling more than 15 million votes.

During the first few years of office, Johnson achieved ratification of an extensive legislative agenda known as "The Great Society" program, which provided legislation to aid education, research to cure disease, Medicare, urban renewal, beautification, conservation, funds to revitalize Appalachia, the poverty-stricken, crime prevention and control of delinquency, and preventing obstacles to the right to vote, such as doing away with literacy tests. He created the Department of Transportation and was a champion of the space exploration program.

Despite his efforts to develop programs to fight poverty and discrimination, two issues plagued the Johnson Administration. Unrest and race riots broke out in black ghettos across the country. Also, controversy over America's involvement in Vietnam reached its peak triggering demonstrations and clashes with police to erupt on college campuses and in the streets of major cities throughout the country.

In his address to the nation in March 1968, Johnson announced a halt to bombings of North Vietnam and stunned the entire country by unexpectedly announcing that he would not seek re-election. He gave the unrest and division within the country over the Vietnam War as a reason, stating that he wanted to devote his full attention to reaching a peace accord instead of being distracted by campaigning. Peace talks were well underway when he left office in 1969, but he did not survive to witness their outcome. He retired to his ranch in Johnson City, Texas, where he suffered from heart problems and died on January 22, 1973.

Jimmy Carter

Thirty-Ninth President
1977-1981

Born: October 1, 1924 in
Plains, Georgia

Married to
Rosalynn Smith Carter

James Earl (Jimmy) Carter, Jr. was born October 1, 1924, in Plains, Georgia, the eldest of four children of a farmer and manager of a small country store in this rural community known for its peanut farming. Jimmy was the first in his family's history to finish high school. He attended the Georgia Institute of Technology for a year before receiving an appointment to the Naval Academy in Annapolis, Maryland, and married his hometown girlfriend, Rosalynn Smith, upon graduation in 1946. They had three sons and a daughter.

Carter spent the next seven years as a naval officer, with the intention of making a career of the Navy. His ambition was to become an admiral. However, when his father died in 1953, Jimmy relinquished his commission and returned to work the family farm. He expanded the business beyond peanut farming into shelling, processing, and warehousing peanuts and became relatively prosperous. By the early 1960s he had developed an interest in state politics and ran for the state Senate in

1962. After losing by a handful of votes, voting irregularities were discovered and Carter challenged the outcome, ending with having the results overturned and him being elected. Eight years later he was elected Governor of Georgia and became one of a new breed of Southern governors who focused on issues of ecology, efficiency in government, and the elimination of racial barriers. While in office, he reduced the number of state agencies from 300 to 22 in an effort to cut down on government waste.

In December 1974, two years before the election, Carter announced his candidacy for President. This gave the relative unknown an opportunity to campaign over an extended period and gradually gain momentum. By the time he arrived at the Democratic National Convention in New York City in 1976, he was a familiar figure and the frontrunner for the Democratic Party. He was nominated on the first ballot. Choosing Senator Walter Mondale of Minnesota as his running mate, Carter campaigned hard against President Gerald Ford and faced off against him during three televised debates. Carter won the election by a margin of 297-241 electoral votes.

One of the biggest issues he faced was the energy crisis. To combat America's dependence on foreign oil, Carter enticed Congress to form the Department of Energy along with legislation to help decrease oil consumption and increase oil production as well as encourage use of other energy avenues. However, inflation and unemployment were the real albatrosses he faced. He called for voluntary limits on wage and price increases, but they had little effect. He entered office with high popularity ratings, but the gasoline shortage combined with ongoing economic problems caused his rating in the polls to reach an all-time low by 1979. Inflation and interest rates were at near record highs. He deregulated the trucking and airline industries, expanded the national park system, including the protection of 103 million acres of land in Alaska, and created the Department of Education.

He made great strides toward peace in the Middle East by bringing together Egyptian and Israeli leaders at Camp David in 1978, leading to the signing of a peace treaty in 1979. He also obtained ratification of the Panama Canal Treaties, established full diplomatic relations with the People's Republic of China, and completed the Salt II nuclear arms agreement with the Soviet Union.

He was forced to meet two critical challenges in 1979. First, Iranian militants seized the U.S. Embassy in Tehran and held Americans hostage. A month later, the Soviets invaded Afghanistan to put down an anti-Communist rebellion. The remainder of his term of office was spent trying to free the hostages and bring sanctions against the Soviet Union for their aggressive acts. When negotiations with Iranian leaders got nowhere, the U.S. halted trade, but the measures didn't work and Carter ordered military action. That, too, failed. Carter's response to the Afghanistan issue was to first limit trade with the Soviets and then call for a boycott of the 1980 Summer Olympic Games in Moscow.

Carter couldn't overcome the consequences of not resolving Iran holding Americans captive. That, combined with the inability to reverse the inflation, led to his being defeated by the Republican challenger, Ronald Reagan, in the 1980 Presidential election. On the day after Carter left office, January 21, 1981, Iran released the 52 U.S. hostages.

William J. Clinton

Forty-Second President
1993-2001

Born: August 19, 1946, in
Hope, Arkansas

Married to
Hillary Rodham Clinton

Bill Clinton was born William Jefferson Blythe IV on August 19, 1946, in Hope, Arkansas. His father was killed in an automobile accident three months before his birth and his mother remarried when he was four. He adopted his stepfather's family name when he was in high school in Little Rock.

An honor student who played the saxophone and was popular with his classmates, young Clinton considered becoming a musician, or perhaps a doctor or reporter, until he visited the White House as part of an American Legion Boys' Nation delegation and shook hands with John F. Kennedy in 1963. Kennedy, who would die from an assassin's bullet just a few months later, made such an impression on him that he decided to pursue a career in politics.

After graduating from high school in 1964, he attended Georgetown University in Washington, D.C. and worked part-time in the office of Senator J. William Fulbright of Arkansas. After receiving a degree in international affairs in 1968, he won a two-year Rhodes scholarship to Oxford University in England. In 1970 he attended Yale University's Law School, taking time off in 1972 to join the presidential campaign of Democratic Senator George McGovern of South Dakota. He received his law degree the following year.

He served briefly as a staff lawyer for the U.S. House of Representatives Judiciary Committee and on the faculty of the University of Arkansas Law School when, in 1974, he ran unsuccessfully for Congress. Although he lost the election against a highly popular and powerful four-term Republican candidate, he showed remarkably well, due in large part to a backlash against Republicans because of President Nixon and the Watergate scandal.

In 1975, he married a girl he met at Yale, Hillary Rodham, who continued to establish a successful law practice in Little Rock. They had one daughter.

He was elected Arkansas' attorney general in 1976 and in 1978 he became the nation's youngest governor when he won the state's top job. He lost a bid for a second term because of a gasoline tax he imposed to improve state highways, but regained the office four years later with three subsequent re-elections until he ran for President in 1992, defeating incumbent George Bush and third party candidate Ross Perot.

The youngest President since JFK immediately set out to establish economic reforms. He called for nearly $500 billion in tax increases and spending cuts and won congressional approval for the North American Free Trade Agreement (NAFTA) with Canada and Mexico.

During Bill Clinton's tenure the U.S. enjoyed more peace and economic well-being than at any time in its history. Despite accusations of misconduct involving real estate investments, sexual harassment, and inappropriate sexual behavior in the White House, Clinton's performance rating was high, especially in relation to the economy. The first Democratic president since Franklin D. Roosevelt to win a second term, he was responsible for the lowest unemployment rate in modern times, the lowest inflation in 30 years, the highest home ownership in the country's history, reduced crime rates in many places, and decreased welfare roles. He proposed the first balanced budget in decades and achieved a budget surplus.

In 1998, Clinton became the second U.S. president to be impeached by the House of Representatives as a result of personal indiscretions with a young female White House intern. After he was tried on charges of perjury and obstruction of justice and found not guilty in the Senate, he publicly apologized and continued to have unprecedented popular approval ratings for his job as president.

He failed to get the health care reforms he wanted, but was more successful in initiating legislation to upgrade education, to protect jobs of parents who must care for sick children, to restrict handgun sales, and to strengthen environmental rules. He called for a great national initiative to end racial discrimination in celebration of the millennium in 2000.

He successfully dispatched peacekeeping forces to war-torn Bosnia and bombed Iraq when Saddam Hussein stopped United Nations inspections for evidence of nuclear, chemical, and biological weapons. The biggest military operation of his presidency was in joining other NATO countries in a massive bombing campaign against Yugoslavia. He helped negotiate a Mideast pact between Israeli and Palestinian leaders, but failed to reach an agreement between Israeli Prime Minister Ehud Barak and Palestinian leader Yasir Arafat on the establishment of a Palestinian state.

In 2000, his wife Hillary became the only First Lady to be elected to the U.S. Senate when she won a seat from the State of New York. After he left the White House, Clinton set up an office in New York City's Harlem where he remains in demand as a speaker and fundraiser.

Democratic National Conventions

1832: Baltimore, MD

1835: Baltimore, MD

1840: Baltimore, MD

1844: Baltimore, MD

1848: Baltimore, MD

1852: Baltimore, MD

1856: Cincinnati, OH

1860: Charleston, SC
    and Baltimore, MD

1864: Chicago, IL

1868: New York, NY

1872: Baltimore, MD

1876: St. Louis, MO

1880: Cincinnati, OH

1884: Chicago, IL

1888: St. Louis, MO

1892: Chicago, IL

1896: Chicago, IL

1900: Kansas City, MO

1904: St. Louis, MO

1908: Denver, CO

1912: Baltimore, MD

1916: St. Louis, MO

1920: San Francisco, CA

1924: New York, NY

1928: Houston, Tex.

1932: Chicago, IL

1936: Philadelphia, Pa.

1940: Chicago, IL

1944: Chicago, IL

1948: Philadelphia, PA

1952: Chicago, IL

1956: Chicago, IL

1960: Los Angeles, CA

1964: Atlantic City, NJ

1968: Chicago, IL

1972: Miami Beach, FL

1976: New York, NY

1980: New York, NY

1984: San Francisco, CA

1988: Atlanta, GA

1992: New York, NY

1996: Chicago, IL

2000: Los Angeles, CA

2004: Boston, MA

Democratic Organizations

(in alphabetical order)

College Democrats of America
430 South Capitol Street, SE
Washington, DC 20003
202-863-8151
collegedems.com

The College Democrats of America (CDA) is the official student outreach arm of the Democratic Party. It aims to elect Democrats, train and engage new generations of progressive activists, and shape the Democratic Party with voices from America's youth. CDA was founded in 1932 to boost the presidential campaign of Franklin Delano Roosevelt. From the 1940s to the 1960s, it was the largest student political organization in the nation.

Democratic Congressional Campaign Committee
430 South Capitol St. SE
Washington, DC 20003
Phone: 202-863-1500
www.democraticaction.org

The Democratic Congressional Campaign Committee (DCCC) serves as the official national Democratic campaign committee charged with recruiting, assisting, funding, and electing Democrats to the U. S. House of Representatives. They provide services ranging from designing and helping execute field operations, to polling, creating radio and television commercials, fundraising, communications, and management consulting.

Democratic Freedom Caucus
demfreedomcaucus@yahoo.com

The Democratic Freedom Caucus (DFC) is a progressive, pro-freedom caucus, which promotes the values that the Democratic Party was founded upon: individual liberty, constitutional democracy, and social responsibility. In supporting the Bill of Rights, which describes what is meant by individual liberty and constitutional limits on government, the DFC advocates progressive, freedom-oriented policies, which emphasize: promoting the public interest rather than favoritism to special interests; building incentives for improving the quality and efficiency of public services; and upholding civil liberties.

Democratic Leadership Council
600 Pennsylvania Ave., SE
Suite 400
Washington, DC 20003
Phone: 202 546-0007
Fax: 202 544-5002

The Democratic Leadership Council is an idea center, catalyst, and national voice for a reform movement that is reshaping American politics by moving it beyond the old left-right debate. New Democrats are the modernizers of the progressive tradition in American politics, believing in the traditional values that have always propelled the Democratic Party and believing that the best way to further those values in a new era is to modernize policies and programs to keep up with the changing times.

Democratic National Headquarters
430 S. Capitol St. SE
Washington, DC 20003
Phone: 202-863-8000

The Democratic National Convention established the Democratic National Committee (DNC) in 1848. The DNC is the oldest continuing party committee in the United States and the world.

The Democratic National Committee plans the Party's quadrennial presidential nominating convention; promotes the election of Party candidates with both technical and financial support; and works with national, state, and local party organizations, elected officials, candidates, and constituencies to respond to the needs and views of the Democratic electorate and the nation.

While anyone who is registered to vote as a Democrat is a member of the Party, there are 440 members of the Democratic National Committee. The National Committee has 9 elected officers: The Chair, five Vice Chairs, Treasurer, Secretary, and National Finance Chair.

Membership on the National Committee is composed of individuals selected by the Democratic Party organizations in each state (including the District of Columbia and Puerto Rico), the U.S. Territories (American Samoa, Guam, and the Virgin Islands), and Democrats living outside the United States.

Each jurisdiction is represented by its Chair and the next highest ranking officer of the opposite sex. An additional 200 votes are distributed to the states and territories based on population, with each receiving a minimum of two additional seats. Each delegation must be equally divided between men and women.

Also seated on the DNC are representatives of various Democratic constituencies and elected officials. These include two U.S. Senators and U.S. Representatives, two members of the College Democrats, and three representatives each from the Democratic Governors, Mayors, State Legislators, County Officials. Municipal Officials, Young Democrats, and the National Federation of Democratic Women. Fifty members are appointed by the DNC Chairmen, and approved by the DNC, and are considered "Members-at-Large."

Democratic Senatorial Campaign Committee (DSCC)
120 Maryland Avenue, NE
Washington, DC 20002
Phone: 202 224-2447
Fax 202 224-3120
Email info@dscc.org

The Democratic Senatorial Campaign Committee (DSCC) is the national committee of the Democratic Party formed to elect Democratic members of the United States Senate. The DSCC enables Democratic candidates to conduct effective campaigns that reach voters and secure the election of a Democratic Senate in the year 2004.

Democratic Underground
P.O. Box 53350
Washington, DC 20009
E-mail@democraticunderground.com

Democratic Underground was founded on Inauguration Day, January 20, 2001, in part to protest the presidency of George W. Bush. Since then, DU has become one of the premier left-wing websites on the Internet, publishing six days a week, while hosting one of the Web's most active left-wing discussion boards.

Democrats Abroad
430 South Capitol St. SE
Washington, DC 20003, USA
Phone: 202 863 8103
Fax: 202 863 8063
info@democratsabroad.org or
webmaster@demoatsabroad.org

Democrats Abroad is the official Democratic Party
organization for some six million American citizens who
live outside the United States. They work to support the
aims and principles of the Democratic Party. They are
recognized as a "state" committee by the Democratic
National Committee and are represented on the DNC by
eight members.

Indiana University College Democrats
900 E. 7th Street
Suite 574
Bloomington, IN 47405
E-mail: iudems@indiana.edu

IUCD is dedicated to promoting the Democratic Party
platform, involving IU students in the Democratic Party,
and to electing Democrats to local, state, and federal
offices.

National Democratic Institute for International Affairs
2030 M Street, NW, Fifth Floor
Washington, DC 20036-3306
Phone: 202 728-5500
Fax: 202 728-5520
Contact@ndi.org

The NDI is a nonprofit organization working to
strengthen and expand democracy worldwide. Calling on

a global network of volunteer experts, NDI provides practical assistance to civic and political leaders advancing democratic values, practices and institutions. NDI works with democrats in every region of the world to build political and civic organizations, safeguard elections, and to promote citizen participation, openness and accountability in government.

National Jewish Democratic Council
P.O. Box 75308
Washington, DC 20013-5308
Phone: 202-216-9060
Fax: 202-216-9061
E-mail: info@njdc.org

Founded in 1990, the National Jewish Democratic Council is the national voice of Jewish Democrats. Informed by our commitment to those values shared by the Democratic Party and the vast majority of American Jews, including the separation of church and state, a strong US-Israel relationship, and reproductive freedom.

National Stonewall Democrats
P.O. Box 9330
Washington, D.C. 20005
Phone: 202 625-1382
Fax: 202 625-1383
field@stonewalldemocrats.org

National Stonewall Democrats (NSD, with more than 70 local chapters, is America's only grassroots Democratic lesbian, gay, bisexual and transgender organization. They address issues of importance to GLBTs within the National Democratic Party. Local Stonewall Democratic Clubs are located throughout the country.

New Democrats On-Line

New Democrats On-Line includes The Democratic Leadership Council (DLC) which leads the New Democrat movement, a national network of elected officials and community leaders whose innovative ideas are modernizing progressive politics for the 21st Century.

Oklahoma Democratic Party
4100 N. Lincoln Blvd.
Oklahoma City, OK 73105
Phone: 405 427-DEMO (3366)
Fax: 405 427-1310
GENERAL E-MAIL: odp@okdemocrats.org

The Democratic Party of Oklahoma reflects the solid values of the state it represents, honesty, hard work and compassion for those who are less fortunate. It views itself as the party squarely in the center of the political spectrum.

Progressive Policy Institute
600 Pennsylvania Ave., SE
Suite 400
Washington, DC 20003
Phone: 202 547-0001
Fax:202 544-5014

The Progressive Policy Institute is a catalyst for political change. Its mission is to modernize progressive politics and government for the Information Age. Leaving behind the stale left-right debates of the industrial era, PPI is a prolific source of "Third Way" thinking that is shaping the emerging politics of the 21st century.

21st Century Democrats
1311 L Street, N.W.
Suite 300
Washington, DC 20005
Phone: 202 626-5620
Fax: 202 347-0956

21st Century Democrats' mission is to promote traditions of the Democratic Party through the election of economically progressive, populist officials who are the next generation of Democratic leadership.

Women's National Democratic Club
1526 New Hampshire Avenue, NW
Washington, DC 20036

WNDC Educational Foundation
1526 New Hampshire Avenue, NW
Washington, DC 20036
www.wndcfoundation.org
Phone: 202-232-7363
Fax: 202-986-2791
info@democraticwoman.org

In 1922, the Women's National Democratic Club was founded in Washington, DC, two years after the 19th Amendment granted voting rights to women. As the first organization for Democratic women in the nation's capital, the club provided a social setting for political dialogue between visiting Democrats and residents of the District who were excluded from national suffrage.

Emily Newell Blair, vice chair of the Democratic National Committee (DNC) in charge of women's affairs, was the principal founder. As a DNC official, Blair oversaw the organization of more than a thousand clubs for Democratic women throughout the country. She also established political schools, hoping to revitalize the party through a well informed women's electorate.

Florence Jaffray "Daisy" Harriman, a Washington and New York socialite, recruited prominent political and social figures for WNDC membership and financial support. Harriman had entered national politics in 1912 to campaign for her friend Woodrow Wilson in his first bid for the U.S. presidency.

Wilson endorsed the club, and former First Lady Edith Bolling Wilson was elected honorary president. Harriman also launched a series of bipartisan Sunday night suppers that raised the Democratic Party profile and quickly became a Washington institution.

In 1924, when WNDC opened its doors in rented quarters near the White House, members recruited influential Washingtonians to speak at club luncheons. The twice-weekly events have endured for nine decades and remain WNDC's most prominent activity.

Young Democrats of America (YDA)
PO Box 77496
Washington, DC 20013-8496
Phone: 202 639-8585
Toll Free: 877 639-8585
Fax: 202 318-3221
E-Mail: office@yda.org

The Young Democrats of America (YDA) has been the official youth arm of the Democratic Party since 1932. Open to anyone under the age of 36 who affiliates with the Democratic Party, YDA is a nationwide grassroots organization with 42 chartered states and 780 local chapters. The 43,000 plus membership reflects the broad diversity of America and the Democratic Party. This includes high school students, college students, young workers, young professionals and young families. All of the members have the interest of their community at heart and work hard to affect the democratic process. YDA works hard to:

- Elect Democratic Candidates
- Encourage youth involvement in the Democratic Party
- Support the ideals of the Democratic Party at all levels of government
- Instill young people with the values for which the Democratic Party stands
- Provide young people with the skills and experiences they will need to lead America

Young Democrats of North Carolina
220 Hillsborough Street
PO Box 12196
Raleigh, NC 27603
(919) 821-2777
Fax: (919) 821-2778
E-mail: info@ydnc.org

Formed in 1928, the Young Democrats of North Carolina is an organization for all registered Democrats from the ages of 18 to 35 who have an active interest in governmental affairs, who are seeking a mechanism for satisfying political expression, and who want to make the members of the Democratic Party aware that young people intend to take an active role in party affairs. The vision of the Young Democrats of North Carolina (YDNC) is to make North Carolina a better place by promoting its issues, its young people, and the spirit of the Democratic Party.

Glossary of Terms

Beauty contest — A preliminary vote usually taken early in the electoral process within a party; it expresses a non-binding preference for one or another of the party's candidates. This preference is not linked to the selection of convention delegates.

Caucus — Literally, it means "a meeting," and it is one of the main mechanisms used by modern American political parties to nominate their candidate for president. In the presidential nomination process, it now denotes a meeting of local party activists at the precinct level who select, in an open forum, delegates to county meetings. These delegates in turn select delegates to state meetings; and these state-level conventions select delegates to the party's national convention. The purpose of this layered caucus system is to open political participation to as many people as possible, and to provide greater incentives to recruitment of fresh talent into party politics than merely voting in a primary election. From February to June of a presidential election year, the major political parties of every state conduct either caucuses or primary elections ("primaries"). By tradition, the rural, Mid-Western state of

Iowa has the first set of caucuses in the nation, even before the first primary in New Hampshire, and so it has a big impact on the race, even though it is a small state with so few delegates.

Conservative — In American politics, someone who is right-of-center politically. Of the two major parties, the Republicans are generally considered more conservative. In the United States, conservatives usually emphasize free-market economic principles and often prefer state and local governmental power to federal power. Traditionally, conservative support has come from business leaders. Candidates and voters commonly refer to themselves and others as conservative, moderate, or liberal.

Convention — A meeting, at state or national level, of "delegates" from a political party. These delegates vote for the person they want their party to nominate for political office. The nominated candidate will then compete in the general election with the candidates of other parties, and against any independent candidates, not endorsed by a political party. In modern U.S. presidential politics, "convention" usually refers to the national conventions of the Democratic and Republican parties, held every four years, during the Summer before the general election which is held in November. These conventions, which include delegates from all states of the Union, the District of Columbia, and U.S. territories, formally nominate the presidential candidate.

Delegate — An official representative selected by members of his or her party to a national or state political convention.

Democratic Party — One of the two current major political parties. For the most part, particularly since the early 1930s, the Democrats have been considered the party of less affluent people, and have supported an activist role for the federal government in the economic and social sectors. The first Democratic president, Andrew Jackson, was elected in 1828, as the seventh U.S. president. The Democratic Party is generally considered to be more liberal or less conservative than the Republican Party.

Electoral base — A politician's "electoral base" is considered to be the heart of his or her constituency, i.e., the groups of people who will usually vote for him or her whatever the prevailing political conditions at any given time, often out of party loyalty (contrast with swing voters), or some other combination of variables such as ethnicity, gender, religion, ideology, military service, geography, or positions on issues. In other countries, "electoral base" is often called the "vote bank."

Electoral College — The Electoral College is the group of electors, chosen by voters throughout the U.S. on a state basis, on Election Day, who then meet and formally select the next president of the United States. The selection is by a majority of 270 votes out of the 538 electors. The Electoral College system is mandated by the U.S. Constitution.

Get-Out-the-Vote ("GOTV") Operations — In the last few days of a campaign, particularly on Election Day, campaigns usually focus most of their resources on getting their electoral base out to the polls to vote. Such operations (abbreviated as "GOTV" by campaign managers) include television and radio broadcasted appeals, telephone banks of volunteers and campaign workers who call voters' homes, reminding them to vote, "soundtrucks" with amplified speakers that drive through neighborhoods of likely supporters, volunteer drivers who drive likely supporters, particularly the elderly or disabled, to the polls, "pollwatchers" who ensure the integrity of polling operations, and dissemination of campaign paraphernalia such as buttons, balloons, brochures, flyers, banners, lawn signs, posters.

GOP — An abbreviation for "Grand Old Party", nickname of the Republican Party.

Independent — In U.S. politics, this term denotes a voter, who, when registering to vote, does not declare affiliation with the Republicans, Democrats, or other political parties or does not consider himself or herself to be a member of a political party. Likewise, the term can also refer to a candidate for office who is running on the basis of personal identity rather than party affiliation.

Liberal — In American politics, "liberals" tend to be people who are somewhat ideologically left-of-center. They tend to favor more power at the federal level and federal intervention to regulate economic issues and certain social issues, particularly social issues involving civil liberties, and the rights of minority groups. Of the two major parties, the Democrats are generally considered more liberal. Traditionally, the bases of liberal support have been among minorities, urban voters, labor unions and academics, though that is evolving as U.S. politics change. Candidates and voters commonly refer to themselves and others as conservative, moderate, or liberal.

Midterm elections — This term refers to elections held between presidential elections, that is, two years after the previous, and two years before the next, presidential elections. Each midterm election selects one-third of the 100 members of the U.S. Senate and all 435 members of the House of Representatives, as well as many state and local officials.

Persuasion activities — Campaigns frame or define a message that will appeal to the undecided voters, and convey that message through advertising (television, radio, and print), direct-mail to the voters' homes, door-to-door and street-corner campaigning by volunteers or campaign workers, personal appearances and speeches by the candidate, candidate appearances at debates, endorsements and testimonials, and favorable coverage in the news, referred to as "free media" because candidates did not have to buy advertising space or time. Campaigns generally do not waste resources attempting to persuade voters that comprise the opposition's electoral base. As for their own electoral base, campaigns generally target get-out-the-vote resources.

Platform — A formal statement of position on major political issues drafted by a candidate or a political party. In other countries, the "platform" may be called the party "manifesto." The major parties ratify their platforms at their national conventions.

Plurality — A plurality of votes is a total vote received by a candidate greater than that received by any opponent but less than a 50 percent majority of the vote. In other words, if one candidate receives 30 percent of the vote, another candidate receives 30 percent of the vote, and a third candidate receives 40 percent, that third candidate has a plurality of the votes, and wins the election. Abraham Lincoln and Bill Clinton are examples of presidents who received a majority of the electoral vote, but only a plurality of the popular vote in a competitive three-way election contest.

Primary — A "closed" primary is a system of selecting a party's candidate for office in an intraparty election in which only registered members of that party may vote. Most state primaries are closed. An "open" primary is a system of selecting a party's candidate for office in which voters registered with other parties and "independent" voters (i.e., unaffiliated with any party) may also vote. This kind of primary is also known as a "cross-over" primary. The major political parties in every state choose delegates for their party's national nominating conventions, by means of either a primary or a caucus. By tradition, the state of New Hampshire has the first primary, soon after the Iowa caucuses, and so it has big impact on setting the stage for the rest of the race, even though it is a small state with so few delegates.

"Reagan Democrats" — Democrats who voted for Ronald Reagan for president during the 1980s. It has become a generic term for swing voters in the Democratic party.

Realignment — In U.S. politics, this term refers to occasional historic shifts of public opinion and voter concerns that either undermine or enhance one or another party's traditional base of support. The term is generally applied to national elections which clearly shift the majority and minority status of the two U.S. major political parties, or which replace one of the two major political parties with one that previously had been a "third party." Realignment may be based on many factors, such as the reaction to party positions on a critical issue of national concern, as was the case with the slavery issue in the 1860s, credit or blame for handling a national crisis, such as the Great Depression of 1929, or substantial changes in the demographic make-up of the voting populace.

Republican Party ("GOP") — One of the two major U.S. political parties. During the 20th century, the Republican Party has generally been the party of more affluent and conservative voters, and has favored economic and social policies that are somewhat less re-distributive than Democratic party policies. The first Republican president was Abraham Lincoln, the 16th U.S. president, elected in 1860. The Republicans emerged in a major party realignment, replacing the now defunct Whig Party as a major U.S. party. The nickname, often used in newspaper headlines or when a commentator wishes to abbreviate, is "GOP" (pronounced gee-oh-pee, not gop) which stands for a now antiquated and little-used term, "grand old party."

RINO — Republicans In Name Only

Straw poll — In modern presidential politics, a non-binding vote, often taken among party activists and usually at a very early stage in a candidate-selection process, to indicate which candidate or candidates are preferred by a local group.

Stump speech — The "standard" speech of a candidate for office, the one he or she is most likely to use, perhaps with slight variations, on normal occasions.

Super Tuesday — Primary elections are often held on Tuesdays, and Super Tuesdays are when primaries and caucuses are held in several states on the same day, with many delegates "up for grabs." If a candidate does particularly well on Super Tuesday, he or she will not only gain many delegates, but also press coverage and momentum. Since Super Tuesdays are seen as big events on the election calendar, they often have a large impact on the perception of where candidates stand in the race, causing front-runners to solidify the perception of their invincibility, or lose ground to other candidates that do better than expected. Often, candidates that have were lagging in the opinion polls, and that failed to do well in the earlier primaries and caucuses, drop out of the race if they fail to do well on Super Tuesday. They also may find it difficult to raise additional campaign funds, because they are portrayed as not having a chance to win the nomination. Therefore, Super Tuesday may serve as the coup de grace on candidates' campaigns that were already in trouble after disappointing showings in the earlier caucuses and primaries, such as Iowa and New Hampshire.

Swing Voters, Ticket Splitters, and Persuadables
"Swing voters" are those that are not always loyal to a particular political party, and therefore are not part of any party's electoral base. They get their name because they might "swing" from one party to the other in different elections. "Ticket Splitters" is another name for swing voters, because many of them will vote for candidates from opposing parties for different offices on the same ballot (e.g., might vote Democratic for President and Republican for Senator, or vice versa). They get their name because they do not necessarily vote for all candidates on the same "ticket" or slate, thus these voters "split" their votes. When swing voters are undecided as to which candidate they will support, they are called "undecideds." Political campaign managers also refer to undecideds as "persuadables," because campaigns concentrate on persuading them,

through various persuasion activities, to vote for their candidate. Campaigns generally consider the opposition's "natural" electoral base as unpersuadable, and consider their own "natural" electoral base as already likely to favor their own candidate. Thus, they do not waste resources on the former, and only "target" the latter for motivation or assistance to vote, called get-out-the-vote operations, on election day. Although swing voters are sometimes referred to as independents, they may be registered members of any political party.

Third party — In the parlance of American politics, "third party" refers to political parties outside the two-party system which are perceived to have a significant base of support. In the 20th century, that has come to mean a party that is not the Republican Party or the Democratic Party and can play some role in influencing the outcome of an election.

Resources

Democratic National Committee
430 S. Capitol St. SE
Washington, DC 20003
Phone: 202-863-8000

Republican National Committee
310 First Street, SE
Washington, DC 20003
Phone: 202. 863.8500
Fax: 202.863.8820
E-mail: info@gop.com

Wikipedia, the free encyclopedia
Free Software Foundation, Inc.
59 Temple Place, Suite 330
Boston, MA 02111-1307 USA
http://en.wikipedia.org

The White House
1600 Pennsylvania Avenue NW
Washington, DC 20500
Comments: 202-456-1111
Switchboard: 202-456-1414
Fax: 202-456-2461
http://www.whitehouse.gov

Bibliography

National Republican Congressional Committee

Republican National Committee

Democratic National Committee

StarGroup International Book Division

For many years StarGroup International has produced books for clients to use as a media or marketing tool. They have also produced several in-house books of their own. *StarGroup Spotlights* is a series of educational books produced by StarGroup International's Book Division.

This venture began as a philanthropic gesture by the company's president, Brenda Star, but unexpectedly sparked a demand that required a major effort to research, compile, and organize information to produce books on a variety of topics.

It started when Brenda, determined to entice parents to encourage their children to read instead of spending so much time in front of television sets, produced a book highlighting *101 Reasons To READ With Your Child*. StarGroup published 5,000 copies and donated them to Palm Beach County. Her philanthropic needs were satisfied ... or so she thought. Requests for copies were made from as far away as the states of Washington and Hawaii. Before long, requests for bulk orders began to arrive. A number of literacy advocates embraced it and the book was soon endorsed by such noted individuals as Art Linkletter, Mark Victor Hansen, successful Texas businessman and Horatio Alger recipient Tom Harken, and the late Dave Thomas among others. Demand for the book continued to grow, but StarGroup lacked the infrastructure to handle fulfillment of individual copies, and resources to underwrite large bulk press runs of additional printings. The book did go into a second printing in January 2001, when, at the request of Kentucky Governor Paul E. Patton, Toyota Motor Manufacturing of Kentucky underwrote the production for circulation among parents of young children in that state.

Then in September 2001 the shock that reverberated around the globe prompted Brenda to once again respond. The remarkable display of American unity following the 911 terrorist attacks, inspired Brenda and her associates to produce *101 Reasons To Be A Proud American*. StarGroup researched, drafted, designed, published, and had the book ready for distribution within six weeks of the tragedy.

It soon became evident that a trend was developing. While discussions about producing a book series were in progress, interest in the existing books continued to mount. Demands for more than a million copies have been received from across the country from Headstart Program teachers, schools, libraries, the National Alliance of Black Educators, and the Palm Beach County School System.

StarGroup determined that it was important to develop a series of educational books on a variety of topics in addition to Reading and American Patriotism. There are currently ten books in the *StarGroup Spotlights* series in print, ten more in development, and more being considered.

For the past two decades StarGroup International has met the needs of clients, ranging from Fortune 500 companies to local businesses and grass-roots organizations. StarGroup offers services in marketing, advertising, public relations, image development and book production.

By developing local, regional, national and international marketing campaigns, StarGroup International helps corporations, businesses, industries and a wide range of professionals send their message to target audiences.

For more information contact

StarGroup International at (561) 547-0667

or visit their website:

http://www.stargroupinternational.com